LIGHT THROUGH PRISON BARS

Jesus.

Loves

you.

Noel Procter

Light Through Prison Bars

JENNY COOKE

KINGSWAY PUBLICATIONS
EASTBOURNE

ISBN 0 85476 491 7

Designed and produced by
Bookprint Creative Services
P.O. Box 827, BN21 3YJ, England for
KINGSWAY PUBLICATIONS LTD
Lottbridge Drove, Eastbourne, E. Sussex BN23 6NT.
Printed in Great Britain.

This book is dedicated to all those who give their time and energy to bring light into prison.

Acknowledgements

Noel and I would like to thank the following people:
  Tony Collins, literary agent
  Francis Cooke, some interviews
  Michael Deaves, formerly of Prison Office Press
    Office
  Edward England, literary agent
  Robin Halward, Governor of Strangeways
  John Hargreaves, Assistant Chaplain-General
  Beryl Pipes, for secretarial work
  Susan, Helen and Rebekah Proctor.

Contents

Author's Preface

Light Through Prison Bars is the second book about Noel Proctor, prison chaplain, and his wife Norma. It is a sequel to the first, *The Cross Behind Bars*, which was published in 1983, and goes on reprinting.

This second book takes Noel and Norma's story on from 1983 to the opening of the new Strangeways prison in 1994. The period of Noel's professional life (1970–1982) is briefly referred to in Chapter 5 and fully covered in *The Cross Behind Bars*. Yet *Light Through Prison Bars* also looks back to Noel's early years in Belfast and to his life as a teenager at home with his parents. Some readers may find this surprising in a sequel, although much of the material is new and only a very few incidents are taken from the first book. I have done this for two reasons: I wanted this second book to stand alone for a new generation of readers, and to show how Noel became the man he is today. And I wanted this story to live again for people who have read and enjoyed the first book, and to remind them of Noel's early life.

Jenny Cooke
October 1995

11

Foreword

I have worked closely with Noel Proctor during two periods of my twenty-one-and-a-half years in Her Majesty's Prison Service, from mid-1984 to mid-1988, when I was Deputy Governor at HMP Manchester, more commonly known as Strangeways, and from September 1992, when I returned to the prison as Governor, until the time of writing this in March 1995.

Noel's impact on the prison community has been and continues to be immense. That community over the years is many thousands strong, embracing as it does prisoners and their families, staff and their families, and all the many visitors who come as professionals or in a voluntary capacity. Yet Noel's influence reaches further still, through newsletters, through videos, through this book and the earlier one (*The Cross Behind Bars*) to the thousands of people who believe that all of us, whether we are connected with prisons or not, have some responsibility towards those in prison— a responsibility which condemns the crime but not the criminal, and in the interests of our society seeks to encourage every prisoner to find a way of life which avoids crime.

Why has Noel made such an impact?

- Because he combines an acceptance of situations and people with a passionate desire for change for the better.
- Because he seeks for and nurtures the good in everyone, with his (as his wife Norma described it in her journal) 'naive faith in human nature'.
- Because of his commitment and sense of duty.
- Because he cares.
- But above all because of his faith. He has had a far from easy life, but his faith has enabled him to cope with everything and has made him ever stronger.

This moving account of Noel and his work cannot fail to inspire all who read it.

I am glad to have this opportunity to thank Noel publicly for all his support and care for me over the years.

Robin Halward
Governor HM Prison Manchester
March 1995

Prologue

Buckingham Palace—9 March 1993

The air struck chill as Noel shut the front door behind him. 'You got everything?' he said in a half-whisper to his two daughters, who were waiting near the car. They looked over to him. 'Come on, Dad. It's freezing.'

'Better not miss the train, Dad.'

Noel grinned. 'Let's be off then. London here we come.'

The three of them climbed into the car and he drove away through the quiet streets to Piccadilly Station.

The bustle of parking, ticket buying, finding seats and sitting down carefully so as not to crease their best clothes was soon over. Noel leaned back and contemplated his two daughters. He was glad Helen and Becky were with him, even though he was sorry Susan had not been able to come as well, because she had an exam to take that day. Who would have thought in the old days that the paper boy from the back streets of Belfast would have fathered such a gang of beautiful girls? Helen caught his eye and he smiled back. Each of them had Norma's red hair, though Susan's was dark, Helen's auburn and Becky's a bright, reddish gold.

'Drink sir?' The British Rail steward hovered at his elbow with a trolley.

Noel started. 'Er, yes. Tea please, if you have it.'

The train gathered speed and raced beyond Stockport and Macclesfield, past gardens of daffodils and through fields greyish-green in the early light. He leaned back and drank the tea. The girls were chattering together and he felt quiet, but quietly excited also. It was going to be a day to treasure; a day in which to let his mind slip back into the past. Norma would have been so thrilled to have been coming with them. And what would his father have said to a son who was at this moment travelling to London to be honoured with the MBE by the Queen at Buckingham Palace? Noel half-smiled as he remembered back to those early teenage years in Roden Street, West Belfast.

Early one evening his father had heaved himself out of the fireside chair in the back room. Noel had sidled in, hoping not to be noticed.

'That you, Noel! Where've yer been?'

'Er, out. Selling papers. Messing about.'

'Oh you have, have you!' And his father rolled up his shirt sleeves until the tattoo on his forearm stood out blue and bulging in the firelight. 'Messing about with that Davey. I told yer. Police were at his house last night!'

'I didn't pinch the bike, Dad, and anyways, Davey's all right and . . . '

'No!' His father unbuckled his belt, holding his trousers up with one hand while the belt flopped in the other. He lowered his head and lurched towards Noel, grabbed him and shook him. 'Don't bring no trouble on this house!' he shouted. 'Remember the hole from which you were dug, lad. Remember it.'

'Yes, Dad.'

There was a short pause. His father sucked his breath in. 'Oh, get on with you!' He pushed Noel away and put the belt back on. Suddenly he swung round and Noel jumped. 'Remember it!'

Now as the train travelled on Noel gazed through the window without seeing the view. Yes, his father would have been pleased and proud of him today. All at once Noel chuckled. Becky touched his arm. 'What are you laughing at, Dad?'

'Oh, I was just thinking how's when my old mum and dad came to London once when I'd passed my exams at the Church Army College. And they were coming to the Commissioning Service and I introduced them to Donald Lynch, the Principal, just too late realising how Dad had left his teeth in a glass by the bed upstairs. He hadn't a bar in his grate! It gave Donald Lynch quite a start, I can tell you!'

They all laughed and Noel relaxed in his seat.

Yes, he had come a long way since those days. His father had spoken more wisely than he knew when he had challenged Noel never to forget his roots: his life's work, his purpose and his meaning had all grown up with him from those hard and communal years in Belfast. His call to serve the Lord as a prison chaplain drew strength and understanding from those early experiences. Norma, his wife, had come from a similar background. She had understood so much, so very much . . .

'Dad?' Helen's voice was urgent.

'Mmm?'

'We'll be there soon. What'll you say if she speaks to you?'

'Who?'

The two girls groaned. 'The Queen, of course!'

'Oh, not to worry. I'll think of something.'

So the three of them got off the train at Euston and took a taxi to Buckingham Palace, chatting excitedly all the way. When its mellowed and columned magnificence came into view they gradually fell silent. As they climbed up the palace steps, mingling with the well-dressed crowd, Noel said to himself, 'Dad, you never thought your son would ever get to this place. Fancy the paper boy from the back streets of Belfast coming here.' He smiled to himself, tongue in cheek. 'I should have brought my cornet and played them all a tune!'

Part One

A Life's Work

'And we know that in all things God works for the good of those who love him, who have been called according to his purpose . . . to be conformed to the likeness of his Son' (Romans 8:28–29).

1

The Cornet

On the 12th July 1947 Noel was up early and joined the Boys' Brigade Brass Band, ready to march in the Orangemen's Parade. All the bands from West Belfast massed until the signal was given and the parade started. They marched for four hours, past narrow streets decorated red, white and blue, with bunting and Union Jacks waving; under the huge wooden archways erected over Sandy Row, with the words 'Remember 1690' and 'King William of Orange' emblazoned on it; past the smouldering remains of bonfires that had burned effigies of the Pope the night before.

Behind the bands came the row of marching Orangemen, each one clutching his black-backed Bible. 'King Billy's Day' meant a day off work, chips and bags of sweets, hazy remembrances of the siege of Derry and the Battle of the Boyne, when the Catholic James 2 of England was finally defeated by the Protestant soldiers, under William, Prince of Orange.

Noel was the solo cornet player in the 46th Old Boys' Band and was kept fairly busy with his music. His friend, Jimmy Robinson, played next to him. Their band leader dropped his baton and gave them a few minutes off playing. Jimmy looked at Noel: 'What's it like living in Roden Street?'

'What d'yer mean?'

'Well, with all them Catholics moving in round yer.'

Noel rested his cornet on his shoulder and rubbed his mouth. 'Well, we live on the Protestant side of the Grosvenor Road, and anyways, most of 'em live in the Falls Road and I'm used to cycling up that way.'

'Why?'

'Well I sell newspapers at the hospital.'

'Which one?'

'Royal Victoria.'

'What they like?' asked Jimmy.

'Who?'

'Catholics.'

'They're all right. We never think of 'em as any different from us. My mum and dad's friendly with all the neighbours and them with us. We never think about what religion they are. Why?'

Jimmy frowned. 'There's no Catholics round us.'

The band leader gave a sign with his baton and Noel raised his cornet to his lips. 'They're all right,' he said.

'Well what you marching for then?' asked Jimmy.

''Cos I'm in the band, you idiot. What you marching for?'

Jimmy grinned. ''Cos I like playing in the brass band.'

So off they went, to a rousing tune and laughter in the crowd; two teenagers, soon lost in the surging marchers and onlookers.

'Noel?'

'What?'

'Do you want to join the Orange Order?'

'Dunno. Do you?'

'Dunno.'

But as the weeks went past Noel began to worry about being in the brass band. He had become interested in Christianity now and surely Christians were supposed to be involved with things like bands and influence their friends to join the church, weren't they? Noel sighed. He could not imagine any of his friends wanting to join the local parish church. 'Always arguing about infant baptism and confirmation,' said his mother.

And then there was the question of joining the Orange Order. They were a nice enough crowd, but he was not sure.

So one Saturday afternoon, after he'd finished playing in the band before the football match began, he went for a cycle to the river. He dropped his ancient bike into the long grass and threw off his jacket. It was hot and the river banks were a mass of dusty dandelions and red campion. He lay down in the grass and listened to a lark singing. All at once he raised himself on one elbow: 'But I don't want to leave the band,' he said to himself. 'I like being in it. I *want* to stay in it.' He lay back again. Playing the cornet was one of the few things he was good at. 'And I like marching in parades and playing at the football matches.'

He could just imagine Jimmy's face if he told him he was leaving. What on earth would the others say? 'Stuck-up!' 'You can't leave. You're the solo cornet player!' 'Flippin' heck!' 'Religious nut!'

Noel stared out across the water. So why was he making all this fuss anyway? It was as if all the time someone were giving him a gentle tug at the elbow and saying in his ear, 'Don't stay in the band. There's nothing wrong with it, but I want you to leave it.'

'Why?' asked Noel. He had been asking 'why' for weeks, and there was still no answer to it. He hauled himself to his feet and flung a stone into the water. It sank at once.

The sun was lower in the sky now and he turned to go. He put his jacket on, picked up the bike from the long grass and then grasped the cornet case. He clam-

bered onto the bike, steering with one hand and carrying his cornet under his other arm. He would have to
hand the cornet in if he left. He grasped it all the
tighter.

He cycled slowly and by the time he got to Roden
Street it was quite late. He cycled past the houses at the
top, past their neat front gardens and red brick walls.
Then he came to his end of the street. They didn't have
gardens. Slowly he got off his bike, cradling the cornet
case in his arms, and opened the front door. He had
made his mind up. He knew what he was going to do.

The following Friday evening there was a band practice. Noel hardly spoke to the family over tea. He was
still smarting from the reaction of the lads at work
when he told them he was not going to the bookie's
at dinner times any more. 'You'll have to place yer own
bets. I'm through with all that now.' There had been
various mutterings of 'kill-joy' and 'religious maniac'.
They didn't send him to Coventry, but they were a bit
cool. He knew they would get over it in time, but he
sighed. Life was becoming rather hard going.

He waited until the band practice was over and then
stood up in the lull while everyone was getting their
breath back.

'There's something I'd like to say.'

But no one took any notice, so he cleared his throat
and tried again. 'I like being in the band, but, er . . .
I'm handing in my resignation.'

'What? When?'

'As from now.'

'What the heck for?'

'Well I'm, er, a Christian now and I feel there's other
things I ought to be doing.'

The silence hung heavy in the air. Noel looked round.
If only someone would say something.

'But you're the solo cornet player!'

Noel bit his lip. 'Yes. I'm sorry.'

'Sorry!'

'Aw come on, Noel. Don't leave.'

'Don't go, Noel.'

They all tried, even Jimmy, to persuade him to stay. But he stuck to his guns. Several of the lads cold-shouldered him on his way past them.

Jack, the band leader, said nothing as Noel handed over the cornet in its case. Jack took it out and examined it closely. It gleamed in the electric light. 'I've taken care of it, sir,' said Noel.

'I can see that,' said Jack. He put the cornet back in its case, and snapped it shut. Then he turned away, and never gave Noel a second glance. Noel hovered for a moment and then turned to go. Out of the corner of his eye he saw Jack shaking his head, and then he was out through the door and into the street.

He walked along, pushing his bike. It felt funny without the cornet case to carry. There was nothing much to do and no one to walk with, so he might as well go home.

He meandered along, one hand thrust deep into his pocket, his shoulders hunched. The bike wobbled over the cobbles in the gutter as he plodded on, one grey stone after another. Idly he kicked at a sweet paper, and it fell down the grid. So what was he going to do at the weekends now? He shrugged and sighed deeply. He heard some footsteps running behind him, but did not bother to look round. Kids chasing, probably.

'Noel! Noel!' He stopped and looked round quickly. Who on earth . . . ? Then he saw Jimmy puffing along down the street, waving to him.

Noel's face lit up. 'Hello, Jimmy.'

'Hello. Can I walk with you?'

'Yes. Course.'

They walked on a bit. Jimmy seemed stuck for words and would not look at Noel. At last Jimmy stopped. 'You'd tremendous courage back there, Noel.'

Noel shrugged. 'Aw, no I hadn't. Anyway, I don't feel very brave now.'

Jimmy drew breath and then his words all came out in a rush. 'Well, I want what you've got!'

'Pardon?'

'I want it.'

Noel stopped dead and his bike scraped on the pavement. 'What?'

'Being a Christian.'

Noel put his hand on Jimmy's shoulder. 'You do?'

'Yes. I made my mind up as I was running after you.'

'Oh Jimmy! That's wonderful!'

They stood together on the pavement, grinning at each other and then shook hands. Noel slapped Jimmy on the back. 'Good for you, mate.'

Jimmy grinned. 'I've left the band too. Tell you what, I'll come and call for you tomorrow afternoon.'

'Shall we go on a bike ride together?'

'Yes. Smashing.'

They went off home in the twilight. Noel held his head high and his eyes shone. He was really glad he had said what he had said after the band practice now.

2

The Hallelujah Postman

The following afternoon Jimmy was round at the Proctors' as soon as dinner was over, his brown eyes bright with excitement.

'Hey, Noel! You'll never guess what!'

'What?'

'My mum says she knows a chap called Billy Johnson.'

'You mean the postman?'

'Yes. He told her about a male voice choir at Sandy Row Methodists. Oh, and he runs meetings and things. So why don't we ask to join the choir?'

Noel chortled and slapped Jimmy on the back. 'Why not indeed!'

'It's not quite as good as the band . . . '

'But it's the next best thing!'

So the two lads cycled off to Sandy Row. As they turned into the Row, they saw a wiry little man getting off his bike outside the Methodist building. Jimmy touched Noel on the arm. 'That's him.' They crossed the road and leaned their bikes against the wall, and then slowly walked over to him. Noel pushed Jimmy in front of him. Jimmy cleared his throat. 'Excuse me, sir, but we'd, er, like to join the, er, choir.'

'Please,' added Noel.

Billy Johnson turned round. His eyes twinkled behind his National Health glasses and he took

Jimmy's hand and shook it for ages. 'Bless you, lads,'
he said. Then he took Noel's hand and pumped it up
and down. 'Well, can you sing, lads?'

'Noel can play the cornet,' blurted out Jimmy and
Noel dug him in the ribs.

'Jimmy played in a band as well, sir.'

Billy ran a hand through his crisp greying hair and
then beckoned them to follow him into the hall at the
side of the church.

Suddenly he swung round: 'But do you know the
Lord?'

Noel and Jimmy halted in their tracks, almost falling
over one another and Jimmy went pink. Noel stepped
forward. 'Yes, sir. We do.'

Billy looked at Jimmy. 'And when did you get to
know the Lord?'

'Last night, sir.'

A smile lit up Billy's face. 'Bless you both.'

They got into the hall and Billy took off his jacket.
'Give us a hand with these tables, will you? We're
having a meeting tonight.' After a while they had all
the tables down one side of the hall and the chairs put
in rows in front of the stage. Billy was whistling 'The
Old Rugged Cross' and the two lads joined in the
chorus, Noel singing tenor and Jimmy, bass.

While they were singing Noel noticed Billy had
stopped whistling and was standing with his head on
one side, listening to them. 'What is it, sir?'

But Billy would only smile and shake his head.
'You're good at singing, you two, aren't you?' was all
he'd say.

Billy brewed some tea and opened a paper bag of
sandwiches and shared them with the lads. They sat
round the rough wooden table together, munching the
potted meat sandwiches and then sucking some treacle
toffees that Jimmy found in his pocket.

Noel listened wide-eyed as Billy told him about what went on at the Methodist church. Night after night was crammed with meetings: the Bible class, the men's meeting, the Saturday night open-airs, the follow-up visiting, the male voice choir practice, the visits made to other churches. And Billy, it seemed, had a hand in them all.

He seemed to grow a bit taller as he told Noel and Jimmy about it all. 'Best thing of all, lads, is the half-night of prayer.'

'The what?'

'We have 'em every now and again after the open-air on a Saturday night. They're wonderful. But,' he wagged a finger at the lads, 'no girls allowed at the half-night of prayer. I'm not having no girls hanging around here after midnight.'

Jimmy smothered a giggle. As if he and Noel were bothered about girls! They sat on at the table, looking up at Billy.

Finally Billy stood up and put his jacket on over his hand-knitted pullover.

'I must be getting along. Shall I see you two again?'

'Oh, yes,' said Noel and Jimmy together.

'And you like singing?'

'Yes.'

'Cheerio then.'

'See you tonight.'

'What a smashing bloke,' said Noel on the way home. 'I wish I was like him.'

'Yes,' said Jimmy. 'My mum says he's always singing "Hallelujah" when he delivers her letters. And if he goes on the bus at weekends, do you know what he does?'

'No.'

'He starts talking about being a Christian to the people he's sitting next to. My mum's seen him.'

Noel was silent and hunched over the handlebars. 'I could never do that.'

'No, neither could I.'

They got to Roden Street. 'See you tonight then.'

'Bye.'

At 8.00pm prompt they were back in the Methodist Hall. Billy and a few lads were singing on the stage and several men were dotted about on the rows of chairs.

'Come on up here!' called Billy, and they stumbled up onto the stage, Noel trying to hide behind Jimmy. It seemed to Noel as if the whole population of Sandy Row was gazing at him. He opened his mouth to sing and no sound came out. He swallowed and tried again. Then an arm came round his shoulders. It was Billy's. 'You're doing fine,' Billy whispered. 'Wonderful voice.' Noel glowed, opened his mouth and sang as he'd never sung before.

When they had finished the hymn, sparse clapping came from the hall. ''Burdens Are Lifted at Calvary'',' called out Billy, and they began to sing again.

As the evening wore on the hall filled up. And after closing time it got really full. One by one, Billy let the singers on the stage have a 'go' at talking about their faith. 'Just for a minute, mind,' he said.

Noel didn't have a notion of how to speak in public. He stuttered and stumbled over the words. 'Well, I once won a Sunday school prize. It was a big black Bible. Inside I read these words: "He who comes to me, I will in no wise cast out." This made an impression on me. Then when I was selling newspapers on the wards at the Royal Victoria I met a man called Mac. He'd had to have thirty-four operations. But he was always cheerful. When I asked him why he'd helped another patient, he said it was because he wanted to. But when I asked him again, he said . . . ' Noel swallowed. 'He said it was because he'd got Jesus in his life. Jesus had given him peace.' Noel stopped. 'Then afterwards, he . . . he died. And then I had a friend—a footballer called Sammy—and he died too. It all made such an impression on me. These deaths. And our Stanley's death, my brother, when I was only a few days old. I couldn't make it out.'

Quite a few men were listening by this time. Noel faltered and then hurried on. 'The Sunday school teacher said you met your Maker when you died. And I realised I'd never talked to God before, so in the end, one night, I knelt down on the bit of mat between the two beds in our back bedroom and asked God if I could be a Christian. Er, that's it.'

Noel stepped back from the mike and hid behind Jimmy. He wiped his forehead with the back of his hand. Phew! Thank goodness that was over.

Billy got the audience singing and clapping, even a tear or two flowed, and then, as if by miracle, everyone was utterly quiet while he prayed.

As he came to the end of his prayer, someone shouted out at the back of the hall, 'Holy Joe!'

'Shut up!' called out several of the men.

Billy stopped praying at once, motioned the singers to sing again and then ran down to the back of the hall.

Noel watched him. How on earth did Billy keep all this lot in order? He could tell a lot of them had rolled in from the pub, and even one or two of his dad's cronies were there. Yet they all sat quietly enough.

Billy was leading a drunk chap back with him. 'You Holy Joe,' sang the drunk.

'Poor old man,' whispered Jimmy. Tattered, torn and smelling, the drunk was led up to the platform.

'We're glad to see Ted here tonight, aren't we?' shouted Billy.

'Yes!' roared the crowd.

'He likes to tease me and call me Holy Joe, but you don't mean it, do you?'

The drunken Ted attempted to shake Billy by the hand. 'No, no,' he said, and swayed very close to the mike. Billy had his arm round Ted, and keeping him upright, turned to the crowd. 'The Lord Jesus is pleased to see Ted here tonight, isn't he?'

'Yes!' roared the crowd.

'And he can utterly change Ted, can't he?'

'Yes!' roared the crowd again, and then they all stood to their feet and sang the closing hymn.

Later, when everyone was going home, Noel noticed Billy take Ted into a back room, and he followed. In the back room Billy was giving Ted strong tea and was washing his face. 'Come on now,' he said and took off his own jacket and put it round the drunk's shoulders. Billy darted round the drunk, preaching to him, cleaning him up, praying for him and giving him tea all at the same time. He glanced up and saw Noel.

'But he can't understand a thing you're saying about putting his trust in the Lord,' said Noel.

Billy sagged for a minute and then brightened up. 'Use every opportunity,' he said and then, 'Do you want to come with me and get him settled for the night?'

Noel nodded.

So Billy put one arm round Ted, and Noel supported him on the other side. Ted let them lead him out, grumbling and grousing all the time.

'Come on, Ted lad,' said Billy. 'There's nothing doing here. Your old cronies can't take you back to their homes. Their missuses wouldn't have it.' So Ted gave in and came with them.

Jimmy Robinson pushed through the crowd at the

door and grabbed Noel's arm. 'Hang on a minute, Noel. I want you to meet Jim Long.'

Noel glanced up, grinned at Jimmy, said 'hello' and shook Jim Long's hand with his left hand. 'See you tomorrow, lads. Sorry I can't stop now. Billy needs me.' Then they plunged outside. It was dark and cool and quiet after the heat and bustle inside.

They walked slowly down the pavement and Ted swayed between them, shuffling along in his dusty hobnail boots. The toe cap was flapping on one and some newspaper was peeping through. Then he stopped and lurched forward. Billy steadied him and propped him against a lamp-post. Ted leaned forward and retched into the gutter, and Billy kept his hand on Ted's shoulder. Noel stood his ground, but turned his head away.

After a bit Ted straightened up; his face was grey and the bristle trembled on his chin. He tried to speak, but the words would not come. Billy put his arm round Ted. 'Don't worry, lad.' And off they went at a snail's pace, until they came to the doss house in Matilda Street.

Noel had heard of the doss house before, but had never been inside. No matter how drunk or how late back any of the menfolk were in Roden Street, their wives always took them in and quietly shut the front door on their misery. Only down-and-outs went to the doss house.

Billy pushed open the door and a bleary-eyed janitor half got up from a wooden chair that looked as if it had seen better days in the schoolroom. Billy took out some silver from his pocket and the coins clinked on the bare table. 'Couple of nights, please, and food as well.' The janitor nodded and waved them past and then turned back to his newspaper. He had obviously seen Billy before.

They went down the passage to a big room at the back. It was cold and smelled. Tramps lay all around, some covered with newspaper, some on dirty sack mattresses. Noel noticed a spare place and they lay Ted down on a mattress there. He started snoring almost at once. Billy undid the laces on his boots and arranged his jacket over him. Noel stared at the jacket. Billy had been wearing it earlier in the evening and now it covered Ted's stained trousers and greenish jumper that was more gaping holes and strands of wool than jumper.

Billy tugged him gently by the arm. 'Come on, lad.' They went out briskly and passed a foul little kitchen. 'Bread and soup,' said Billy and jerked his thumb in the direction of the grease-spattered kitchen.

Then they were in the street again and the fresh air was sweet. Billy sighed. 'The doss house is grim, but it's better than nothing.' They walked on in silence for a bit. 'That's why I make such a stand against alcohol,' said Billy suddenly. Noel thought about his dad and nodded. 'If I once touch a drop all them men who come every week, they'd laugh at me.' Billy sighed again. 'I know some of 'em laughs at me anyway, but it's a different kind of laugh, and anyways, I don't mind. If I can point 'em towards Jesus, I don't mind. And they know where to come when they're in trouble.'

Noel looked at Billy's white shirt sleeves and hand-knitted pullover. 'Are you cold?'

Billy laughed. 'I've got a good missus. If I don't get my jacket back,' he shrugged, 'I'll have to do a bit of overtime and buy another.'

They came back to Sandy Row for their bikes and Billy stopped and shook Noel by the hand for a long time. 'Well lad, goodnight. Do you want to come to Sandy Row tomorrow morning?'

Noel hesitated. 'I usually go to the parish church, but I could miss it.'

Billy shook his head. 'No lad, that's not the way. There's always the open-air on Saturday night. Shall I see you next week?'

'Yes, rather.'

'Cheerio then.'

'Cheerio, and thanks.'

Noel stood and watched Billy until he had cycled round the corner of the street. Then he climbed onto his bike and cycled home slowly. He was tired but glad, even though his arm ached from supporting Ted. He whistled to himself. Billy was just grand.

3

The Call

One Friday evening Jimmy Robinson called for Noel as usual and they cycled off two abreast for Sandy Row. All of a sudden Noel slowed up. 'What's that noise?'

Jimmy listened. 'It's music, I think. Or is it someone speaking?'

They rounded the corner, then saw a crowd of men and boys clustered round a small rostrum. A girl was speaking into the mike, and behind her were two other girls and a few lads. Noel did not know any of the young people on the rostrum.

'What on earth . . . ?'

'Redeemed Testimony Band,' muttered Jimmy.

'What?'

'Baptist.' They leaned their bikes against the nearest garden wall and inched into the crowd. The girl who was speaking was taller than the other two. Noel gazed at her, oblivious of all the pushing, shoving and whistles. He watched as first her scarlet coat swung round, and then swung back again. She gripped the mike with both hands and was rather pale. Hanging from under her red coat was a froth of white lace. 'Bet she don't know her underskirt's showing,' giggled a lad next to Noel.

'Shut up!' he replied so fiercely that the lad moved off. Then she started to speak again, her voice quaver-

36

ing slightly. Noel gazed at her dark hair, burnished with red lights. 'Who's that?' he asked Jimmy.

'Jim Long's sister.'

'Who?'

'You know, you've met him at Sandy Row.'

'Oh yes.'

Jimmy was serious. 'Would you like to meet her?'

Noel shrugged. 'If you like.' He took care not to be seen staring at the girl again. Yet he made sure he was near Jim Long when the clapping died down and the group began to pack up their things.

'This is Norma,' said Jim Long. 'And Eileen and Christine, her friends.'

'How do you do?' said Noel, looking at Norma.

Norma tossed her head. 'Pleased to meet you.' Then she and the other two girls burst into a fit of giggles and Noel went pink.

'Come on, you lot,' said Jimmy. 'Let's go and see if Billy's about.'

Norma hung back and touched her brother on the arm. 'Who's that awful chap?'

Jim Long looked surprised. 'Noel Proctor. He's all right.' Jim stroked his chin. 'I thought I'd invite him to the Christian Endeavour Society. Do you mind?'

'Mind? I'll never go again.'

But she and Eileen and Christine were there the very next Monday. Noel was the star of the evening. He sang a solo and then led the chorus-singing. He did all the actions to all the words and sang all the choruses twice. The people there loved it. All except Norma and Eileen and Christine, who sat on the back row.

'Isn't he awful!' said Norma in a low voice and sat on her hands. 'I'll *not* do any of those actions!'

Eileen grinned. 'He's coming over.'

Norma started flicking through her Bible, pretending not to notice him. Noel cleared his throat. 'Hello.'

Norma tossed her glowing hair. 'Hello, Noel.'

'There's just something I wanted to tell you. It's about last Friday evening.'

Norma tensed and looked up. 'Did I speak all right?'

Noel grinned. 'Great. You were very brave.'

Norma shrugged.

'Yes you were.' Then Noel was serious. 'But did you know your underskirt was showing?'

'Well, really!' said Norma on the way home. 'Isn't he the limit? Who does he think he is?'

Her brother chortled in the darkness. 'Well you'd better get used to him, 'cos he's coming to Christian Endeavour every week now. He's been asked to be on the Look-Out committee. If anyone can ginger up Christian Endeavour, he can.'

Norma groaned. 'Oh no!' And she and Christine and Eileen burst into fits of laughter.

So life continued for Noel, with his job as a cloth-cutter at Philips and Jones during the day, and most evenings spent at meetings or singing in the male voice choir. Yet underneath this busyness a longing grew within him, until it was like a voice calling him each day, very quiet but quite insistent. The call was not clear cut, but it had to do with his wanting to be like Billy; wanting to make something out of his life; wanting to get along-side the lads and men he knew so well in among the back streets, factories, churches and red-brick terraces of West Belfast. He wanted to tell them about Jesus; that there was something more to life than working so hard all week that they had to get drunk every Saturday night in order to forget it all.

He read deeply, particularly influenced by two books he had bought from the second-hand bookstall. One was about John Fletcher of Madeley, who had worn away his floorboards with his constant praying. The

other was called *Helps to Holiness* by Commissioner
Brengle of the Salvation Army.

In the end he became confused. Was God calling him
to be like Billy and reach the men round him? Or to be
like John Fletcher and be holy? Or to seek the power of
the Holy Spirit like Brengle said? Or was God calling
him to be a missionary?

He saw himself standing by a campfire in the jungle,
with his Sunday school prize Bible in one hand. He was
proclaiming with the other, making a huge embracing
gesture, and somehow he seemed taller than all the
Africans who were clustered shyly in the bushes. He
preached his heart out: 'Repent . . . come to the Lord
Jesus . . . be baptised . . . ' And they came, brown eyes
trusting, and crowded round him, understanding the
brash attempts he made at their language.

Noel closed his eyes. He could just imagine telling
Billy. Yes, it was a lovely dream and perhaps one day. . .

The back door crashed downstairs. So it must be
after 10.30pm and his dad had come home pretty
well-oiled as usual. Noel could hear him muttering
downstairs and then his slow, heavy tread upstairs.
He paused on the tiny landing, hiccuped and then
lurched into the front bedroom. Noel frowned in the
darkness. Really, his dad was getting too bad these
days. *Thank goodness I don't drink*, he thought.

He kept hearing the mumble of voices in his parents'
bedroom and then their door opened. His mother was
talking and then his dad said, 'First you moaning at
me, and now there's that hypocrite son of mine who's
always condemning me.' His dad flung his shoes onto
the landing and they fell with a thump against the wall.
Then the door slammed.

Noel lay very still for a long time. He tried to get to
sleep, but couldn't. The dream about being a missionary in the jungle shrank and shrank until it seemed to

fall into pieces round him. *How can I be a missionary if I can't even win my own dad?* he thought. The darkness was very still. It seemed to Noel as if he caught a whisper in the dark bedroom. 'How can you win your dad if you don't love him? If you don't forgive him? If you don't respect him?'

Noel sat up and then got out of bed. He pulled open the drawer of his chest and got out a hankie and blew his nose. After a while he rubbed his eyes. The trouble was, as fast as he rubbed them, they were wet again. He got back into bed again and thought for a bit. He knew what he would have to do. He shut his eyes and whispered, 'I'm sorry, Lord. I've made a right mess of things. I've been rotten about my dad.' He rubbed his eyes again. 'I don't know how to . . . please help me to talk to him . . . I really do want to respect him.' He lay quiet again and this time a sense of peace stole over him and he fell asleep.

It was quite late when he got home from work the next day, but his dad was back early from the pub. Noel wandered across the back room. 'Where's Mum?'

'In the parlour. At it again.'

'Stanley's photo?'

'Yes.'

Noel fell silent for a moment. His mother had never forgotten Stanley, the son who had died of diphtheria a few days after Noel was born. Even now she often stood in the parlour and gazed at his photograph for what seemed like hours. Then he said, 'Dad?'

'What?'

Noel swallowed and fixed his eyes on the hob. The words tumbled out. 'Dad, I want to go into full-time Christian work. I've thought a lot about it. I'd have to leave Philips and Jones and perhaps go to college or something.'

His dad sat dead still, gazing at the fire. Noel moved a step nearer. The words he wanted to say kept sticking in his throat, but he took a deep breath and forced them out. 'But, Dad, I want your blessing on it.'

There! It was said now. Silence hung between them in the back room, and then his dad's chair creaked as he struggled to get up. His eyes glinted in the firelight and he too seemed to have difficulty in getting his words out. Finally he said, 'Lad, I never thought you'd come and even talk to the likes of me about a thing like that.' He wiped his eyes with the back of his hand.

Noel went pink. His dad turned his head away and used the back of his hand again. 'I told her. I told your mum, "You'll be proud of that lad one day. You'll see."' He turned to face Noel again. 'You broke your legs often enough when you was small, but you're strong enough now. Bigger 'an me.'

Noel grinned. 'You wouldn't mind then?'

'Mind? No I would not!'

Noel grabbed his father by the hand and shook it hard, and then turned and ran upstairs two at a time. He felt warm all over, and in his heart he was singing as loud as he could.

Eventually Noel went to night school, passed his exams and was offered a place at the Church Army College in London, which he accepted. It was hard saying goodbye to so many friends and family; hard to leave them and the work they had shared behind.

Somehow, until that firm offer of a place came, he had not been quite sure he would get to London. So he had not said much about it to Billy and the others. They knew, of course, but as he would only be away a few weeks at a time, the break perhaps would not be very noticeable. He had seen Billy looking at him a time or two though. And Noel knew the break was coming.

It was the Saturday of the Orangemen's Parade and Noel wandered to Sandy Row and saw Billy watching the procession and went up to join him. He did not see Noel at first. Noel swallowed and then touched Billy on the arm. Billy swung round and his face lit up. He shook Noel by the hand. 'Hello there, lad. How are you?' He turned and gestured to the marchers. 'Look at 'em all, Noel. All carrying a Bible.'

'Yes, Billy, I . . . '

'Aren't you glad you left the band now, Noel?'

'Yes, but I . . . '

'I was so proud of you when you decided not to march with the parade.'

'I'm not against them, Billy.'

'No, I know you aren't. And neither am I, lad. They're our countrymen.' Billy stood proudly to attention as the strains of 'God Save Our Gracious Queen' floated past. 'An' I'm proud to be British. But what I says, lad, is, "Does what you do bring people to Jesus? Does marching with the Orangemen honour Jesus Christ?" An' if it don't, there's no point in belonging to it, is there?' Billy stood back. His eyes were bright. Men in the crowd kept waving to him. Noel had a lump in his throat. All those men. And Billy had won so many for Christ.

'Billy?'

He turned, 'Yes?'

'I'm leaving.'

Billy stared at the ground. 'When?'

'In September.'

They were silent.

'I'm going to college in London. It's definite.' But Billy did not clap him on the back like his father had done or scurry round telling people, like his mother had done. Billy just looked up at Noel. 'I suppose I had heard about it. Well, you're a man now.' His shoulders sagged and he sighed. Then he looked up and said, 'You wouldn't think of not going . . . and sharing the leadership with me?'

But before Noel could answer, Billy shook his head. 'No, no. It wouldn't do. You go, lad.' He paused. 'I just wish that . . . ' He didn't finish, but turned and strode over to the church hall.

Noel followed him. 'I'll only be gone two years. And there's holidays. I'll be back then and be able to help you.'

But Billy did not look at him. He just put his hand on Noel's shoulder. 'Goodbye, lad.'

Noel stopped. 'But look here, I've not gone yet.'

Billy chuckled. 'Of course you haven't. Come on in and meet some new recruits.' Inside the hall was a knot of young lads. They were all about seventeen. They clustered round Billy, gazing up at him, their eyes bright, while he explained about the visiting scheme.

Noel hung back. Everything he knew, he had learned from Billy: how to visit the sick, to pray with them, to give up all his spare time, to lead a meeting, to preach, to testify. That was why he had put off telling Billy. He realised it now. He could not bear the hurt look veiled behind Billy's jokes.

So what was wrong with staying here, helping Billy, earning good money at Philips and Jones? He could go to Christian Endeavour with Jimmy, Jim Long, Norma, Eileen and Christine. It was just that he felt excited about going to London. And on top of that, there was the same insistent, gentle tug to go. He had felt it before—the night he had left the band, and even before that, on the night long ago when he had prayed to become a Christian. He knew. He *had* to go to London.

He looked round the little hall and smiled. It held
good memories. But he had to go on. He looked at the
lads clustered round Billy who was standing in the
middle of them, all gazing up at him. He turned
slowly, half-raised his hand in farewell, and went out
and pushed his way through the crowds towards home.

On the way home he met Norma. 'Hello there.'

'Hello, Noel.'

They stood looking at each other for a moment and
then sat down together on a garden wall. Norma put
her head on one side.

'What's this I hear about you going to college, Noel?'

'Yes, I am. In September. Church Army, in London.'

Norma smiled at him. 'That's wonderful.' She
wriggled her foot and then looked directly at him.
'I'm really pleased for you. I wish I could go to college.'

'Well, why don't you?'

'It's no good. I'm like you were. I left school at
fourteen, I've no "O" levels and I've got a good job
at the Post Office. My mum's a widow.'

Noel nodded. He understood all right. 'It'll come,
Norma. You've got to trust. The Lord'll bring it about.'

Norma giggled. 'You never miss an opportunity, do
you?'

'I beg your pardon?'

'To bring the Lord in!'

Noel went red. 'I am *not* always bringing him in!'

Norma patted his arm. 'Sorry, I didn't mean it really.
You've lots more nerve than me.'

Noel glanced at her. 'Will you take over my job as
leader on the Look-Out committee?'

Norma's eyes opened wide. 'Me? But I'm no good at
singing!'

Noel chuckled. 'You'd have to lead the choruses, *and*
use your hands for the actions. No more hiding on the
back row giggling at me.'

Norma flushed and Noel went on, 'I know I look funny.'

'You do *not*.'

Noel glanced at her. 'Oh thanks. By the way, can I write to you? About Christian Endeavour I mean.'

Norma said, 'Yes, all right. But I can't guarantee any replies. Well, I will reply, but not straight away.'

They got up to go. 'Shall I see you home?' asked Noel.

Norma shook her head. 'No, I'm on my way to Christine's.'

'Cheerio then.'

'Cheerio.'

Noel watched her go through the crowd, her red hair glinting in the sunlight. She was all right, was Norma.

4

And the Bike Came too

The years at college were a challenge. Noel found he enjoyed practising speaking at Hyde Park corner, but life with the other students was not quite so straight-forward. Somehow he did not feel as if he fitted in; as if he did not belong to a world where you called the others 'students' and not 'the lads'. However, he was determined, settled down eventually and in June 1957 passed his exams with credits. He was commissioned as a captain in the Church Army and promised to serve for five years in the Durham Diocese.

It was while he was on the train coming home for a fortnight's holiday after the end of his course that he realised how much he was looking forward to seeing Norma again. *I'm twenty-seven and I've never had a proper girlfriend*, he thought. All the other girls he knew were all right, but were nothing compared to her. Every week she had written to him and he had replied. She had been so faithful in that letter writing. So, so lovely. His face grew pink as he thought about her. *I'm going to say something to her*, he decided. *The first night I see her, I'm going to speak.*

When Noel arrived home his mother and father made a great fuss of him, and so did Robert, his younger brother. Every evening he had invitations to speak and at nearly every meeting he saw Norma. But she was always at the other end of the room, or if they did start talking, her brother, and Jimmy Robinson, and Eileen and Christine were always clustered round them.

In the end it was the last night of the holidays and he still had not spoken to her. He arrived early at Jimmy Fowler's and soon all the Christian Endeavour gang were there. They talked and laughed and sang and ate. Noel kept glancing at Norma. She was wearing a big collar on her dress and an artificial velvet rose was pinned at her neck. She did not seem to notice him, but sparkled and laughed a lot. All too soon it was time to go home again and still he had not spoken.

Suddenly he thrust himself through the group and touched her on the sleeve. She turned round. Noel fixed his eyes on the rose. 'Can I see you home?'

'Thanks very much. Oh, but I always walk home with Eileen and Christine.'

'Oh, that's all right. I'll see them home too.'

The four of them set off walking home, Noel nearest the kerb, pushing his bike. First they saw Eileen home and Norma waited for him to say goodbye as well. But he said nothing, just doggedly pushed his bike along, his other hand thrust deep into his pocket. What on earth was he doing? At last they got to Christine's home in Sandy Row.

'Goodnight, Chris.'

'Goodnight.'

That just left the two of them and they walked all the way back to Norma's house. At last they got there.

'Well, goodnight,' said Norma.

'Wait a minute.' He leaned against his bike and his face was in shadow.

'What is it?'

'Well, there's just something I want to ask you, but first of all I'd better tell you . . . '

'What?'

Noel swallowed and took a deep breath. 'I love you.'

Norma stared at him. Her heart gave an enormous leap. It could not be true that Noel, the kingpin of Christian Endeavour, loved her.

She took a step nearer to him. 'Well I . . . '

But he interrupted her, his words tumbling out and jumbled up in his eagerness. 'You see, I'd like to marry you, only I've promised Church Army I'll work for them for five years, so I don't suppose you'd want to wait that long and I'm only home every six months, but if you did want to wait, I'll wait for you because you're the only girl I've had any dealings with, the only girl I've ever liked and now I know I love you, so will you marry me?'

The words hung in the air between them, opening up a whole new life to Norma, so bright, so unexpected, it sparkled like diamonds.

'Oh yes,' she breathed.

'Yes?'

'Yes. Yes. I feel the same about you. I think I love you.'

Noel took her hand. 'Do you really mean it?'

'Oh yes. I realised how much I missed you when you went to college. I couldn't understand at first, but when I realised, I said "goodbye" to my other boyfriend.'

They stared at each other. Noel held onto her hand tightly.

'I waited till tonight to ask you, in case you said, "Get lost!"'

'Oh no,' wailed Norma, remembering. 'You go back to Durham tomorrow.'

'I'll come round and see your mother first thing in the morning. Then we'll get engaged.'

'Engaged,' whispered Norma and clasped her hands

together. Then she said, 'By the way, who do you think you are? Jacob or someone?'

Noel flushed and then said, 'Well, you're not Leah anyway!'

'Who am I?'

'The most beautiful girl in the world.'

At last they said goodnight. Just as he was leaving she started to laugh and pointed to his bone-shaker of a bike. 'Did you have to propose leaning on your bike?'

'Well I needed the support!'

'And the bike came too!'

And so they parted. Noel cycled home, his heart bursting with song.

In her bedroom Norma lay awake a long time. She did not want to go to sleep in case she woke up and found it was all a dream.

But next morning she was just finishing her breakfast, when there was a knock at the front door. Her mother went to answer it and then she heard Noel's voice in the hallway. She swallowed her cup of tea and tried to sit still. She pushed her hands into her pockets and then took them out again. She jumped up, patted her hair, whirled round and then straightened her collar.

Suddenly the door opened and her mother led Noel into the room. 'Well,' said her mother. 'What's all this I've been hearing about you and Noel then?'

Norma blushed and opened her mouth, but Noel cut in quickly. 'I've explained everything to Mrs Long, I mean your mum, Norma, and she's very pleased.'

Mrs Long put her arm round Norma. 'I'm very pleased. Noel will be just right for you.'

Then her mother popped out of the room and he came and sat by Norma. 'I've got you a present,' he said and gave her a brown paper parcel. Norma opened it and the paper dropped unnoticed to the floor. Inside lay a brand new book: *Revelation* by J. B. Phillips. 'Oh, thank you!' she cried and looked at him shyly.

'Open it.'

Inside he'd written, 'With love from Noel.'

Later he had to dash for the boat to Liverpool. 'Write?'

'Of course.'

'See you at Christmas.' She watched him go cycling at speed down her road. At the corner he turned and waved. She waved back and then went indoors. If she wrote to him straight away, he would get it on Monday.

Their lives settled into a pattern: they saw each other every six months. While they were together they were in love, but when they had to be apart, they had to accept it, each believing the other to be called to put God and the job they were doing first.

Norma left the Post Office and was accepted by Musgrave Park Hospital for her nurse's training. 'I remember thinking all the way through the park on my first morning that I would never pass my exams,' she wrote to Noel. 'But I did. And now I've just got some wonderful news. I've won the prize for the exam in surgery! Fancy me, Dumdum, coming first! God is good, isn't he?'

Norma's letters were full of stories of the people she had nursed, of being late off duty so she could just see to that extra last patient. He was proud of her. She was really making something of her life. It was good that he had not pressed her to get married sooner and forget the idea of nursing. She was so obviously right for it.

As the five years of Church Army life drew to a close, Noel began to wonder what to do next. He loved life with the Church Army as he was his own boss. But he was not quite satisfied.

As he thought over his adult life, it seemed like one

long meeting, one long appeal, one long line of folk wanting to know more about Jesus, all interspersed with himself singing a solo, or playing the cornet, standing on soap boxes or beaches or narrow streets. He sighed and got up to make a pot of tea; he liked the life, yes, and he knew in his heart of hearts what his life was about. He was an evangelist. He rolled the word round his tongue. An evangelist.

He stared at the cup of tea and drank slowly. He had wanted to succeed, and he had. He had wanted God's power for service, and God had graciously given it to him. He had wanted to be like Billy, to make something of himself, to get off the big wheel that sucked you down, like had happened to so many of his mates when he had been a youngster in the tough end of Belfast. Where were they now? Some were in prison, he knew. A lot probably got drunk on Saturday nights, like their old dads had done before them. God had helped him, even though he did not deserve it.

He finished off the tea and then prayed, 'What do you want me to do?' The nagging thought that had kept coming back to him over the last few months, nudged at his sleeve again. He pushed it away hastily, knowing even as he did so that he was going to have to face it. 'Get ordained! In the Church of England! Oh no!' He would have to go to college again . . . and poor Norma had waited long enough. He had no money saved, and anyway he liked being his own man.

But by the end of the week Noel had decided: yes, he would go to theological college and get ordained. Norma was wonderful. 'I've still got a bit to go to complete my SRN. So perhaps it's best,' she said on the phone. 'And anyway, you'll be nearer to Belfast. Only a hop across the water from Birkenhead.'

'Could you get me a summer holiday job at the hospital? Then I can start saving up to get married.'

Norma was silent for a moment. 'Yes, as long as it's not Musgrave Park!'

'Why not?'

'Well, I'd not like to fall out with you over a patient!'

Noel was silent and then began to laugh. 'Well, what about the Royal Victoria?'

'I'll do my best.'

And so it was arranged. Noel would work every summer vacation at the Royal Victoria as a porter.

The two years at Birkenhead (1962–64) went by in fits and starts. Noel studied hard under Michael Hennel, burned the midnight oil, and ended up with a distinction in Old Testament studies, the only one in his year. Norma passed her SRN and was a staff nurse at Musgrave Park. They were able to see each other more often, but that made the waiting all the harder, and the settling down in between seeing each other all the more difficult.

One day Noel saw Norma off at the docks in Liverpool and she was very upset. 'I can't stand leaving you again. I'm getting too old. I'm sick of this waiting.' And she hung her head. Then she sailed away, a tiny hunched figure on the deck of the boat, gazing at the strip of water separating them.

He watched her go, heard the ship's horn and saw the seagulls flocking round the ship's stern. *Easy for them*, he thought, and jabbed at a stone with his foot. *They can fly*. He turned and strode away, his collar turned up against the wind, hands thrust deep into his pockets. He had decided what to do.

A few days later he rang her up. 'Hello, darling. Guess what! We can fix a date!'

'What? When?'

'Easter Tuesday any good?'

'But that's so near . . . yes, marvellous! But how did you manage it?'

'I wrote to the bishop and told him we *were* getting married then.' Noel swallowed and his voice fell. 'But er, Norma . . . '

'Yes?'

'I'll have to come back and do my finals here, in June.'

He waited, miserably aware of the tiny pause on the phone. Then she said, 'I don't care. It'll only be eight weeks and I can finish off at the hospital properly. We'll be married then anyway. Oh, it'll be lovely!'

Noel let out a gasp. He had wondered if she would be upset, but she was chatting on about a dress and whatnot.

'I've got plans for the honeymoon too!'

'Oh you have, have you!'

'Yes, a fortnight at Harriet and Derek's guest house in Dun-Laoghaire.'

'Oh, what a lovely idea! All the spring flowers'll be out.'

'Better take an umbrella as well!'

'Oh shut up!'

So they were married on 31st March 1964, and had a wonderful day. It seemed no time at all before Noel was back from college, working as a temporary porter at the Royal Victoria. He and Norma enjoyed those few months of summer before he was ordained at Michaelmas in Durham Cathedral. Their first home was at Haughton-le-Skerne where Noel was curate. Later he became Vicar of Byers Green, near Bishop Auckland. Their first two daughters, Susan and Helen, were born to them in these years, and the family thrived.

One day Noel was invited to speak at a mission meeting in Durham jail. The meeting went well and

Noel enjoyed it. Although he did not know it at the time, this turned out to be the start of twenty-five years as a prison chaplain in British prisons. This was to be a new chapter in their lives, which was to bring challenge, joy and unexpected heart-searching to them both.

5

Prisons of the Mind
1970–1988

Whenever Noel looked back over his life in the early years of prison chaplaincy work, his first few months at Wandsworth stood out as a happy prelude to the harder times they were to have at Eastchurch Open Prison. It was at Eastchurch that a succession of tragedies rocked the family until each day became more difficult for Noel to drag himself through.

As a result of the shock suffered after an IRA bomb blast only streets away from Noel's parents' house, his father died of a heart attack in Belfast. Noel flew over to see him, but was a few hours too late. By the time his mother opened the door and took him upstairs, his father was already dead. Then Norma's mother had a stroke and needed to come and live with them at Eastchurch. Norma struggled to look after her, but the strain was too much. Norma had a miscarriage and this loss of a child affected both Noel and Norma deeply.

However, they weathered these losses. Life settled down, Norma eventually had another baby girl, Becky, and everyone was happier for a while. Then one day, old Mrs Long died peacefully in her sleep. After the funeral, when they should have been trying to pick up the pieces and look forward to the future,

Norma was feeding the baby, white-faced. 'At least Mum never knew,' she said. Noel looked across at her and then down again. 'No,' he said. 'No.' Old Mrs Long never did know that Norma had found a lump in her breast one day while breast feeding. This was diagnosed as cancer and Norma was now undergoing radiotherapy.

It was a severe blow to them, a time when their faith was tested to the limits. Yet Norma clung to the belief that the God whom she loved and served would grant her the life and strength to raise their three daughters to adulthood. Noel found this experience hard to come to terms with. 'Something in me died then,' he was to say later. 'There were so many deaths to cope with. And then the cancer.' It was a bitter search for him to rediscover faith and to rediscover the power of Jesus Christ. Yet in their different ways they both did rediscover this and their faith grew stronger than before.

Noel went to Dartmoor as Chaplain in 1974 and spent five gruelling but satisfying years there. In retrospect the mist and snow seemed to last most of the year. The prisoners he worked with were hardened men. However, he had the satisfaction of seeing the numbers at chaplaincy services rising from eight to about a hundred men. Despite the isolation of 'the Moor' and the incessant wind, Norma did well physically and was pronounced clear of the cancer at each of her six-monthly check-ups.

In 1979 Noel moved to Strangeways Prison in Manchester, where he was made Senior Chaplain and where he remains in the post until retirement. It was here that he was challenged to work in a team with Ian Ferguson from the Church Army and Alf Hughes, the Catholic priest, who were full time at the prison; and Garth Rogers, the part-time Methodist chaplain. There were several assistant chaplains as well, who spent part of their working week with the chaplaincy team.

As the work developed, the chaplains were seeing over half the prison population coming to the several different services on a Sunday. Over eight hundred men were attending church or chapel. As Strangeways had a rolling population of prisoners, many were allocated to other prisons and sent on from there, so those attending services were not the same eight hundred each week. In spite of the tension, pressures and long hours, Noel loved the work as chaplain, preacher, evangelist and 'bridge-builder', forming relationships with prisoners and staff.

In 1983 Norma was pronounced clear of cancer and discharged from Christie's Hospital. The whole family was delighted and relieved. Things were good at work too: Noel felt revival was on the point of breaking out in the prison. Both Noel and Norma were full of hope and enthusiasm for the future. *The Cross Behind Bars* was published and opened the doors for a wider speaking ministry in which they were both involved. Norma returned to nursing full time as a Sister, and began to accept speaking engagements in the area, often talking about Christian healing at these evenings. At the prison chaplaincy a network of prayer partners, churches, prison visitors, clergy and other interested people slowly built up, to support the chaplaincy team.

At the centre of it all was Noel, pouring his heart out into the tough work he loved so much. Day after day he saw much to encourage and challenge him. By the nature of things, of course, some days were harder and less encouraging than others.

One morning Noel walked briskly from the Adult Wing towards the Punishment Block, or the Segregation Unit as they now called it. The bunch of keys was heavy at his waist and jangled slightly as he walked. He never knew who would be waiting for him in the cells, nor what to expect from these daily visits. He unlocked the first cell door and called out, 'Are you all right?'

There was no reply. So Noel stepped further inside and glanced round. A man was sitting, round-shouldered and head hanging, near the window. Clear morning light came through the bars and cheered Noel. It was apparently making no difference to the prisoner.

'Mr Clark, isn't it?' asked Noel.

The head moved an assent.

'Are you all right? Can I get you anything?'

There was no response. Noel looked round the cell. It was oppressively tidy. There were no books, no personal touches.

'I don't think we've talked before,' said Noel, carrying on in spite of the obvious body language from Mr Clark, which spoke as loudly as any words, telling him to go away. 'I'm always ready and willing to listen if that helps. There are books I can get you from the chaplains' library. If you need me to make a phone call, or get the Probation Service to speak to your family, I can do that for you.'

There was a slight quiver across the man's shoulders, but he remained silent.

'I expect you've already had visits from the Governor, the Chief Officer, the MO and the Hospital Officer today.'

There was no reply. Noel waited. 'I'll see you tomorrow,' he said finally. Then he turned to go. He walked back out onto the landing and locked the cell door behind him. The officer on duty was walking towards him. 'Hello, Noel.'

'Hello there.'

The officer nodded towards the locked cell. 'Get anywhere with him?'

Noel shook his head. 'Nowhere at all. He wouldn't even turn round.'

The officer shook his head.

'What's he been sent down for?'

'Oh, stealing from another prisoner's cell. And not for the first time.'

'He obviously isn't very happy in here.'

The officer frowned. 'If Clark breaks prison rules he can take what's coming to him,' he said tartly.

Noel grinned and moved on to the next cell. He went through the same routine, only this time the prisoner was more relaxed, and more polite. However, the response was the same: not really interested in a visit from someone representing organised religion.

He made nine cell visits in total that morning, to nine men who were all very different. Each one had broken prison rules, either by fighting, giving streams of verbal abuse, stealing or refusing to co-operate, and then being confrontational, often ending up by hitting a prisoner or an officer. Their punishment was twenty-three hours a day alone in a cell in the Segregation Unit, with one hour a day only for exercise in the yard. The problem with lending books too was that many a time a man would shake his head at the offer, and Noel knew it was because he could not read. It was so hard to reach these men, and yet the chaplain was in a unique position. He had all the keys and could wander from cell to cell. Men got to know him and at times they would talk. Noel had learned to listen and found that by letting them talk, they could often find the answer to their own problems. Sometimes he would pray with them. Sometimes they wept. Often he felt he was a buffer, a safety-valve between their angers, strains, and frustrations with the prison system. If a wife was ill in hospital or a girlfriend pregnant, Noel could organise a phone call and then come back with any news.

These visits were never easy, but they were part of a chaplain's statutory daily duties. On very rare occasions a man went on protest and made his cell almost uninhabitable by plastering the walls with his own excreta. The smell was unbearable. Fortunately no one had done that for some time now.

Sometimes, however, a man did respond. Noel opened the last cell door. 'Hello there, Derek.'

Derek turned round and smiled at Noel. 'Hello, Mr Proctor. Nice to see you.'

'And how's it with you today? I thought you'd gone back to the wing yesterday afternoon?'

The smile faded a little. Derek shrugged his shoulders and half-turned away. Noel came into the cell. He sat on the only chair and said gently, 'Are you in more trouble, Derek?'

Derek hung his head. He was a slightly-built man with short sandy hair and appeared much younger than his mid-twenties.

'Have you been shouting your mouth off again?'

The young man nodded.

Noel sighed. 'Do you want to talk about it?'

Derek spun round and said, 'I didn't mean no harm. It's just that the words come tumbling out of my mouth. I get so mad, I can't help it. And besides, that lad was having a go at me in the dinner queue.'

'Look,' said Noel, 'it's not the first time you've let your temper get the better of you, is it? Why can't you let the other lads alone? They only try and wind you up. And they succeed. Look at you now. Back in here again. Banged up on your own for twenty-three hours a day and all because you didn't take my anti-swearing tablets.'

Derek half-grinned and took one of the mints Noel was offering him. The atmosphere relaxed.

'Yes,' he said simply. 'You're right.'

Noel tried to size him up. He liked Derek, but he also knew that there was only so much he could do for him in this situation. He guessed Derek had thumped someone in the dinner queue. His fists and his having always to have the last word were Derek's own two worst enemies. He was constantly in and out of the Punishment Block on account of his temper. *He's a prisoner of his temper really*, thought Noel. And it was a temper that was even harder to control than usual, as he was getting over his alcoholism.

'How long have you got this time?' he asked.

'Ten days,' said Derek.

'Oh.' He paused, then—'Would you like some books from the chaplains' library?'

Derek considered this. 'OK.'

Noel made a note in his diary. 'I'll come back and see you later.'

'Ta. Thanks, Mr Proctor.'

Noel let himself out, locking the cell behind him. He wondered what it must be like in there for twenty-three hours. No radios were allowed. Only you yourself and your thoughts. And books if you could read. One hour walking round and round the exercise yard, and even that depended on the weather. The only views were high, rearing red-brick walls, with their rows of tiny barred windows. There was the industrial landscape against the skyline, but virtually not a tree to be seen. Some small areas of grass and plants grew around the prison and that improved matters slightly. Pigeons and starlings flew about and some men tried to feed them and make pets of them on the windowsills. This was not allowed, but officers often turned a blind eye to it.

Noel walked on to the Hospital Wing and made his rounds there. He frequently sat at a sick prisoner's bedside and this seemed to calm them. He knew he could call on one of the many prison visitors if a man was in need of human contact, and visits could be arranged. There were many men with psychological problems in prison. So much of his work was in listening. Often men were unsure of themselves in prison. It was a new environment and their emotions built up—sometimes to illness point, and they ended up in the prison hospital; sometimes into aggression, when they would wreck their cells and end up in the Punishment Block.

He looked at his watch and hurried on. The Governor had called a meeting about the new Home Office initiative called Fresh Start. As Noel listened, he realised that Fresh Start was going to sweep right through the Prison Service. Prison was to be a more caring place. It was to be a community prison, changing for the better. Many classes and groups which had closed down due to industrial action, were to restart. The government was to put in more money. Overtime for prison officers was to stop, in favour of a thirty-nine-hour week and a reasonable wage. Staff quarters too would now charge rent, or staff could buy their own houses. Noel's brow puckered. As soon as he mentioned that to Norma she would say she wanted them to buy their own house. And perhaps she was right. It would be something of their very own and she would love it, he knew that.

Afterwards he spoke to the Governor. 'Won't these changes mean smaller staffing at weekends?' said Noel.

The Governor agreed with him. 'I hope it'll work,' he said. 'I am very hopeful. And I'm keen to implement it all and get going on education and workshops.'

'And my classes—men's society, confirmation classes, choir, prayer . . . '

'Yes, yes,' said the Governor and laughed. 'You can carry on with your classes. Do you ever stop, Noel?'

'Er, well.' He considered it. 'My wife says I take the

pressure home at times, but she doesn't mind. She listens to me and then I make her a cup of tea! Then I listen to her and then we both put each other right!'

Later that afternoon Noel considered his day. There had been prayers at 7.45am in the chaplaincy, followed by reception. Here the chaplains interviewed every man or boy who had been sent down the night before. They worked in a team with the senior officer on duty, the probation officer, the Education Service and the industrial manager. Often these prisoners were anxious and Noel's job was to reassure them and then, if they wished, let their family know where they were.

Then he had done the Punishment Block, hospital visits, and more visits. He had taken books to Derek, who had been rather depressed that afternoon. There were classes this evening. It had been a full day, but Noel was at peace with himself. As he spent a few quiet moments with a cup of tea, he thought about prison. So many people were in prisons, not just of bricks and mortar, but prisons of the mind; prisons of their own personality, of fear of the future and insecurity, fear of life itself and the fear of not being able to cope. It was his job to show them the way forward, to point them to Christ who had died to set prisoners free. Of course such men had committed serious crimes and had to pay the price and take the punishment. That was only right. But no one could really be released from the prisons of the mind, apart from by the grace offered by God. And that applied to people on the outside as much as on the inside. Such grace was offered to all people, as Noel knew, but not everyone wanted it. The Holy Spirit never forced himself on people.

Yet in these days he was seeing a movement of the Spirit in the prison. He took a long drink of tea and relaxed in his chair. His work was hard, there was no doubt about that. But how he loved it.

6

The Street Preacher

In the days that followed, Noel visited Derek in the Punishment Block each day. He lent him books and listened as Derek talked. *Yes*, thought Noel, *he is a lad who'll always need to have the last word. Best if I listen and let him get it all off his chest.* He could see that Derek was sizing him up, waiting to ask a question, but unsure of how to put it. In spite of a torrent of words somehow Derek never quite got to the point.

Then one morning Derek said, with rather a flush in his cheeks, 'Can you get me a Bible?'

Noel looked at him 'Yes, all right. I'll bring it down when I can.'

'Ta.'

Noel took it to him later on in the afternoon. Inwardly he was shaking his head. He did not expect a character like Derek to change, even if he wanted to. In the life outside he was too used to alcohol and to shouting with mouth and fists for any change to come easily. Nevertheless, Noel gave him the Bible. 'Here you are, lad. Don't forget to read it.'

'I won't.'

Next morning, as soon as Noel opened Derek's cell door, he said, 'Mr Proctor, I've been thinking.'

Noel waited.

'I've been thinking. And the thing is, well I mean . . .'

For once he seemed stuck for words. Then out they came in a rush. 'What's my life all about? And how can I straighten it all out?'

'Well, lad . . . ' But Noel did not get chance to finish.

'Because I'd like to commit my life to Jesus.'

Noel sat down on the bunk. 'Look, Derek,' he said, 'let me give it to you straight. I respect you for what you are saying and I don't doubt you mean well—at the moment.' Derek made as if to speak, but Noel moved his hand authoritatively and Derek sank back onto his chair again. 'You see if you really mean it and really mean business with God, talk isn't enough. There's got to be action as well.'

Derek hung his head. Then he sprang up again. 'But I want to, I want . . . '

Noel sighed and said gently, 'If you become a follower of Jesus Christ, you'd have to give up your drinking. It wouldn't be easy. Could you do that? And you'd have to learn how to calm down and not let your tongue run away with you.'

Derek said nothing. He looked at his knees for some moments. Then he raised his head and his body went still. 'I want to, Mr Proctor. I want to.'

Noel smiled. 'All right then, lad. Once you are back on the Wings you can join in one of the groups. Maybe the choir. If you're so good at talking you might be good at singing!'

Derek jumped up and ran to the barred window. 'Ta, Mr Proctor.'

Noel let himself out, and locked the cell behind him. He walked steadily away, but inside he felt a little sad. He did not doubt the sincerity of the lad at all. But what would happen to Derek once he left prison and went back to his existence of wandering the streets? He had no roots, no family to speak of. He had nothing

going for him. Anyway, Noel decided he would have to
do as much as he could for Derek while he was inside.

At home that evening he found Norma on the telephone. She waved at him and he went on into the
kitchen for a cup of tea. Charlie, the Yorkshire terrier, gave a yap and raced for the door, sensing a
walk. Norma flew into the kitchen. 'Hello, darling.
Just hang on. Back in a minute.' She grabbed the wall
calendar and rushed out. Noel sat down and waited,
knowing before she came back what it would be. He
heard the phone go down and immediately it started
ringing again. At last she came in, her face alight and
her hands full of calendar and paper, envelopes and a
pen.

'Oh Noel, that's the third invitation tonight.'

He looked up at her. 'To speak?'

'Yes.' She clasped her hands. 'I so want to do it, Noel.
It's ladies' groups, Women's Aglow, Christian View-
point, all in the area. People have read *The Cross
Behind Bars* and so many either have cancer or know
someone who's got it. And they want me to give a
talk about it and tell them how the Lord helped me.
Well, both of us really. And to offer prayers for
healing.'

'What are you waiting for then? Come on, let's take
Charlie for a walk and you can tell me all about it.'

So arm in arm they set off. Norma said, 'Isn't it
amazing how all that we lived through at Eastchurch
and me nearly dying, has had this kind of a resurrection? It's wonderful. So wonderful.'

He squeezed her arm. 'And now I'm going to invite
you to come with me for a change and give your
testimony at a meeting.'

'Oh?'

'Yes. The Independent Methodists are having their

Annual Meeting at a room in Manchester University. And . . .' he paused.

She stopped, waiting for him to go on. When he didn't, she picked up a stick and hurled it for Charlie. 'Well, do go on.'

He grinned. 'And they want it to be on the ministry of healing!'

She chuckled. 'I'm with you, Noel. I'll do it.'

Derek was discharged from the Segregation Unit and moved back onto the Wings again. His behaviour settled down and he kept clear of trouble. Noel spent many sessions with him in the weeks that followed. Derek studied the Emmaus Bible Correspondence Course and was eventually granted a certificate when he passed. The day finally came for his discharge. Noel shook his hand. 'God bless you, Derek. Keep rejoicing. And keep that Bible I gave you!'

'Oh yes, Mr Proctor, I will. Ta. I'll be all right now. I know I will. And ta for everything.'

After Derek had gone, Noel wondered about his future. Would such a lad manage to stay out of trouble? In spite of Derek's jaunty air, Noel knew he had never mentioned a family, or a home, or a job. Noel sighed, prayed for a moment, and then set off on his rounds again.

When Noel spoke at rallies and meetings he tried to explain about the movement of the Spirit in the prison that was happening during these years. Men were committing their lives to Christ through the testimony of cell mates. As he prayed in chapel with Ian Ferguson for groups of men, and they laid hands upon them, men would slip to the floor, touched by the power of the Holy Spirit. On one occasion Noel felt the wind of the Spirit so powerfully that he was caused to stagger

under the weight of it. Some men were speaking in
tongues during meetings. A Muslim officer came and
asked him about two young men who were praising
God and speaking in tongues in the prison showers.
'And,' he said, 'they weren't speaking any language
used where I come from!' Some prisoners who had
committed serious offences were granted the peace
and joy to live quietly in the Segregation Unit, and
then on the Wings, still witnessing as the years
passed. Hundreds, as had always happened, came to
the many Sunday services.

A man called Peter tried to commit suicide, but the
sheets he had knotted together tore at the last minute
and he fell unharmed to the ground. He was over-
whelmed with darkness and remorse because he had
murdered his girlfriend in a rage. Months passed and
he had no freedom from his conscience. He lived in a
state of dark terror, fearful he was going to die. In spite
of a lot of prayer he remained in this condition, even
sleeping under his bed because he was in protest at the
psychiatric help being offered to him. Nothing helped.
Then one day he asked to see Noel, saying, 'Last night I
was under my bed again. It was pitch dark in the cell. I
couldn't sleep. All at once I noticed this light. There
was light all round me, a gentle light. It shone around
me and reached me where I was lying under the bed.'

Noel was quite speechless.

In great calmness and quietness of spirit and de-
meanour Peter went on: 'I thought it must be Jesus.'

Noel bent his head and worshipped God.

Since his release Peter has lived a decent life and
become a church caretaker.

So the stories of blessing, forgiveness, repentance and
peace multiplied in what some in that tough, rough and
hard place of Strangeways called 'the human warehouse'.

When Noel and Norma ministered together at meetings outside of the prison, there were also conversions and healings. An elderly man with a hearing aid announced that he no longer needed it because he could now hear. They saw the goitre on the neck of one woman shrink rapidly and disappear. A girl who had suffered greatly with eczema, cycled round to the prison and waited outside to tell Noel, shyly, that she had been completely cured.

James was in prison for burglary. One day he saw a man whom he did not know walking at the end of the Wing corridor. As soon as James saw this man he said to himself, 'I know I must find forgiveness.' Afterwards he could find no reason why he had thought in such a way. Later on he discovered the man was called Noel Proctor and that Noel could point him to the one and only source of true forgiveness. James found that the forgiveness of Christ was so real that in the ten subsequent years he has not been in trouble with the police again. He married his girlfriend and has given their four children a stable home. It is hard to go straight when there is no glamour and no instant access to a chaplaincy team. Yet James and his wife have managed it.

Another lad called Mark decided to become a Christian, even though he had been a robber all his life. After some time in prison he was ready to accept the words in the Bible which say, 'Let him that stole steal no more.' He admitted a series of thefts to the police, and because he would not give the names of his two accomplices, the judge decided that he alone would have to serve the sentences of all three men. The headlines in *The Manchester Evening News* said 'Born-again convict admits to robbery'. But Mark said, 'Now at least I can live with myself.'

A man called Bob Sutton had a vision for a New Life

Centre in Stockport, used to house and help ex-offenders. He had to work through many problems and difficulties, but eventually his vision has become a reality. Joe Whelan is a field officer for the Langley House Trust. There are the Adullam Homes and a house in Plymouth Grove. All these initiatives were part of the movement of the Spirit in the North West.

Over 5,000 prayer letters were being sent out each month. There were prison visitors and many interested people all over the North West giving, and helping ex-offenders.

In the midst of all this activity, both inside and outside the prison, Noel began to receive some post-cards. He studied the picture on one of them and turned it over to see which city this was. 'Oxford' he read. He sucked his lower lip for a moment and then propped the card up next to the others: Cardiff, Swansea, Bournemouth, Eastbourne. It was amazing how Derek had got about. Once he had come up to Manchester and met Noel for lunch. Noel had watched him afterwards as he had tramped into St Anne's Square, with a sandwich board at his front and back. He had stopped dead in the middle and preached the gospel, the sandwich boards telling the same story too. Noel had been surprised. Many would see Derek as a figure of fun, a caricature of the Bible preacher. And yet Derek, who had no roots, was wandering from town to town, using the one big talent he had. He always had liked talking and shouting his mouth off. Now, thought Noel, the man was using his mouth for God, preaching his heart out for British shopping crowds.

Derek's wandering life of a street evangelist had lasted now for several years. At times he phoned Noel for advice and support; especially when he had ups and downs. He often lived a fortnight at a time in

Salvation Army hostels and these addresses would then entitle him to DSS money.

One day the phone rang in Noel's office. He picked it up. 'Hello there.'

'Oh hello. My name is Nigel Sharp. I'm from Radio Wiltshire.'

'Oh yes!'

'Do you know a Derek Smith, an ex-prisoner?'

Noel was cautious. 'Er yes.'

'Would you be willing to say a few words about him on a live radio phone-in tomorrow evening?' The interviewer then went on to explain the story and left Noel chuckling.

'Right,' said Noel eventually. 'I'll be happy to join you by phone on the programme.'

The evening came and Noel was ready and waiting by the phone when it rang. Also linked to the programme was a bishop. The interviewer began with the bishop. 'Can you tell us what happened to you recently in Oxford?'

'Yes,' said the beautifully articulated voice. 'It was my day off and I was going into the town centre by bus. I wasn't wearing a dog collar. Once in the centre I caught sight of a young man wearing a sandwich board, and I could hear him shouting out about Jesus. I pushed my way through the small crowd of onlookers and decided to challenge him. "Surely," I said, "You don't believe all this stuff about the Christian message. It's 2,000 years old." Well, the man drew himself up to his full height, which wasn't very tall, and said, "I was in Strangeways Prison and I was an alcoholic. Jesus Christ came into my life and saved me and changed my life." He paused for breath and I tried to speak, but he rushed on. "And now I preach the gospel and Her Majesty gives me DSS money to buy tracts to give to people like you!" With that, he rammed the tract into my hand!'

Later on the bishop had gone home and rung up the radio station. 'In all my years as a minister of the gospel, I don't think I've ever been as challenged as I was by that naïve and ignorant young man who told me Jesus loved me. I came home and I said, "Oh God, give me some of the zeal and enthusiasm that young man has got."'

The interviewer then asked Noel to chat to Derek, which he did. 'Derek's a street preacher,' said Noel to the radio listeners, 'who became a Christian in the Punishment Block at Strangeways Prison.'

Now Derek has lots of contacts in many towns. Local church people often give him a bed for the night. The last time he spoke to Noel, some eight years after his conversion experience, he said he would like to think of settling down, and gave Noel the same address as before in South Wales.

Noel and Norma were happy and busy—he in his prison work, she as a Sister at Heathlands Nursing Home and a speaker at many meetings. The Lord was blessing them so much. It seemed as if nothing could come and spoil their happiness in his work, each other and the girls. 'Why,' said Norma, 'next year is our Silver Wedding Anniversary.' Her face lit up and her laughter encircled the room. It seemed that 1989 was going to be their highlight year.

7

The Highlight Year

1989

The 31st March 1989 was a special day in the Proctor household. 'Fancy us being married for twenty-five years,' said Noel as he got up that morning.

'Well, you aren't grumbling, are you?' said Norma tartly as she sat up in bed.

He grinned. 'What do you think!'

'Twenty-five years ago today,' she said, remembering, and her voice softened. 'Oh Noel, haven't we got a lot to be thankful for?'

'Yes, we have. And if I don't nip downstairs and get you that cup of tea, neither of us will ever get going!'

She smiled, and as he ran downstairs her laughter followed him.

The day passed by in a crackle of excitement. By early evening the whole family was assembled at the Christian World Centre in Deansgate, Manchester, where they greeted the 100 guests to their Silver Wedding Anniversary celebration. Noel's brother Tom and his wife had come over from Canada for the occasion, and this was cause for a joyful reunion. Everyone joined in a communion service first, led by Tom Johns, a colleague, and then they sat down to a meal together. Noel and Norma both spoke, followed by Susan singing, Helen playing her clarinet and Rebekah saying a few words about her parents. In the end it seemed as if nearly everyone got up and said something.

Much later that evening, just before Noel and Norma settled down for the night, he looked at the plaque which his mother-in-law had given them as an engagement present, and which was hanging over their bed.

Norma followed his gaze and read the verse out loud: "'All things work together for good to them that love God." That's why it's been so special for us today, isn't it, Noel?'

'Yes. It's been very very special.'

They looked at each other, remembering the past.

Norma said, 'When I was told I had cancer in 1973 and that the prognosis was poor, it seemed as if we would never see this day together.'

He took her hand. 'It has been a very precious anniversary. We've had all these years together. Years we never thought we'd have.'

'And we've been able to see our three girls grow up and encourage them in the careers they want to take up. Noel, isn't it amazing how much God has given us in these extra years? So much we would never have realised about in life, if I hadn't had cancer. My ministry has sprung out of it. Noel, I really do thank the Lord, with all my heart.'

'And so do I,' he said. 'Every day together has been a bonus.'

In July of the same year the chaplaincy work of many years came to a culmination. A mission was planned centring around some videos relayed from the Billy Graham Mission in London. Thirty missioners came from all denominations of the Christian faith, along with some prison visitors and other helpers. They were given permission to scatter around the prison from 8 o'clock in the morning to 8 o'clock at night, visiting and speaking to men in the exercise yard, in the workshops, and wandering at will around the wings.

Many prisoners who normally never came to chapel were affected by the atmosphere in the prison and came to some of the meetings. By the end of the week over 1,300 men had seen the videos and heard the challenge to commit their lives to Christ. Men in the prison hospital and also in the Segregation Unit were able to see them. One evening over half the Rule 43 prisoners (those vulnerable because of their offences) who had watched Billy Graham, stayed behind for counselling.

Catholic priests, Methodist ministers, Anglicans, Baptists, Pentecostals, Salvationists and others all worked together to bring the gospel to the prisoners. One evening, in a quiet moment, Noel realised what a wonderful experience it all was. Many of the prison officers were saying quite openly that the whole atmosphere of the prison had changed. There was a peace there that had come in and calmed many men.

Those men who signed a card were followed up by their own local minister from outside. Inside, Noel and his team were running twenty-nine services and classes each week. It was a time of tremendous blessing and encouragement.

In November a video called *From Crime to Christ* was made of four men who had committed their lives to Christ in prison and who are now in full-time Christian work. The Governor decided that it should be played every morning on reception, as new inmates were waiting to be interviewed, so that they could gain an insight into the alternative to a life of crime.

But one Sunday afternoon in November 1989 a film was being shown in the chapel to the remand prisoners. As the film ended the prisoners remained seated. Within a few moments it became obvious that they had planned and were now putting into practice a sit-down protest. Over 200 men were refusing to leave the chapel, and the officers on duty knew that this was potentially serious and confrontational. Eventually one of the Governors went in and negotiated with them. He promised to listen to their complaints about conditions if they found a spokesman and then left the chapel quietly. In the end the men went back to their cells.

When Noel heard about it he shook his head. An officer said to him, 'There's trouble brewing. I don't like it.'

'Yes,' said Noel. 'I agree. It's worrying.' But then in the general rush of meetings the fact of the sit-down protest slipped to the back of his mind.

Soon the year which had brought Noel and Norma so much happiness, both in the family and in the prison work, was drawing to a close. Christmas preparations were well underway. Noel's birthday on the 23rd December passed, and he had got his trumpet down ready to play carols early on Christmas morning before breakfast in the prison. He joked with Norma about it the day before. 'They keep asking me when I'm going to play. And I know what'll happen when I do. Some of them will shout from behind the cell doors, "More! More!" and some of them will be saying something quite different!'

For once she did not laugh. 'Do I look all right, Noel?' she asked.

He stared at her non-plussed. He nearly said, 'You always look all right. You always look the same to me,' but managed not to, just in time. He studied her and saw she was wearing a flowered dress and a short coat. Her hair glowed with red lights and her cheeks were pink. She really did look the picture of health and smartness. 'You look simply great,' he said.

She smiled faintly. 'Thank you.'

'Come on then.'

They set off in the car and made their way to Elmwood Church near Hope Hospital in Salford, where they were to be guest speakers at the Christmas Eve service. Once inside the new building Norma's face seemed to light up as she took in the Christmas decorations, lights and the tree. Noel glanced at her on the platform. She had been a bit quiet in the car, but then sometimes women were like that for no reason. She caught his eye and smiled encouragingly. He grinned back. So that was all right then. She was quite happy.

He poured himself into a gospel message and finally drew to a close. 'I'd like to introduce you to the one who keeps me on the straight and narrow,' he said, amid laughter from the audience. 'Let me introduce you to my wife. When I joined the Prison Service, you know what they said? They said, "You've joined the Prison Service to get away from the women in your life." I've got three daughters and a wife. The only other fellow in the house is a dog, and he's a bit of an old woman too! Anyway, it's lovely to share the platform tonight with the one who gives me the encouragement. Norma!' There was a burst of applause as he sat down. Norma stood up and stared out momentarily at the people.

As he listened to her, Noel was surprised. Her voice was soft and she enunciated the words slowly. 'Christmas for me means "Christ with us". A Christ who recognises our frailties because he was man as well as God. I was born in the city of Belfast, which you will know from my accent, and I was born again when I was thirteen, through seeing the changed life of a school friend.' Her voice became breathless and tremulous, and she paused. 'Although we look back to our beginnings we also need to think, "What does Christ mean to me today?" Sometimes people think Christians have a natural immunity to life's problems.' She took a quick intake of breath, and then her voice and gaze became intent. 'But Jesus never promised us that, did he? But he did promise his presence with us in life's problems.' She paused again.

Noel began to wonder if she had a headache and whether he should take over. She seemed to be labouring under some strong emotion, and yet she looked so lovely and confident. She began speaking again and he sat back in his seat.

'Life was good to us. We lived in Eastchurch. Things started going wrong there, but joy and sorrow are very much part and parcel of our lives. In the joy of our third child came great sorrow when I discovered that I had a breast lump that was diagnosed as cancer. As a nursing Sister I thought cancer only happened to the people I nursed.' There was a long pause. 'Cancer didn't happen to me. But here I was faced with the fact of cancer and an unknown future. When we married and left home my mother gave us a text from our family home which she knew was my favourite: Romans 8:28, "All things work together for good to them that love God."

'There were times when I wanted to break the glass round the plaque and underline in red "ALL THINGS"—even cancer? Could that possibly work for my good? I was absolutely shocked to learn that I could die and could leave my three children of eight, five and four months old—but I wasn't quite prepared for how Noel would react to my diagnosis. He went totally to pieces and became very embittered and rebellious, and he questioned God's dealings with us as a family. Oh yes, he's an ordained minister, but he's got great big feet of clay. And he was rebellious against God.

'You know, God moves very mysteriously in our lives. As if having cancer was not enough, two days after I came out of hospital while I waited to have twenty-five treatments of radiotherapy, my mother had a second stroke and died. What was God trying to tell me? He was knocking from me all the props I had ever known: the prop of my good health, the prop of my mother's love, the prop of my husband's spirituality. They had all gone. And I was to learn again total and absolute dependence upon him.

'On the Sunday Noel was asked to preach at a Baptist church in Sittingbourne and he rang the pastor and asked to be excused. He said he had nothing to give. Something in him had died and he couldn't be a hypocrite. The pastor encouraged us to come and Noel said to him, "Well, do you believe in the laying on of hands for healing?" And he said he did. And Noel said, "Will you minister to Norma for physical healing and will you minister to me for spiritual healing?" And after the service we were both ministered to by the deacon and pastor of that church.

'On the way home Noel said that he needed a sign from God that I was going to live. He needed a sign that I was healed. I thought this was rather a bold thing to say. But Noel was like a drowning man and he needed something to take hold of.'

Noel listened as she spoke, her voice quicker and lighter now. The old sparkle was back and he knew everything was all right now. He heard her retell the story of how she had read the verse in John's Gospel, 'This sickness is not unto death', and had believed it applied to her own situation. 'I held on to this verse,' she cried, her voice strong and powerful, 'even when I still had to have twenty-five treatments of radiotherapy, and I still had to go every three months, six months, twelve months, for check-ups. But gradually God let me see the whole of the promise that he'd given me. "This sickness is not unto death but that the Son of God might be glorified."'

Her voice broke suddenly and Noel saw her hands were gripping the table. 'I realised that God had healed me for his glory. That is why I am on this platform tonight: because I want to glorify Jesus Christ.' Her voice halted again. Then she carried on: 'I want not to be seen, but I want the healing power of God to be manifest in this church tonight, and realise that although "cancer" is a word we are terrified of, the name of Jesus is greater than the name of cancer.' She paused again. 'And I cling on to the promise of God. Many people say to me quite candidly, "Why do you think you are still alive, when God has taken people like David Watson, and many others?" I am still alive because my ministry is not complete, and when it is, then he will take me as well.' Her voice quivered. 'I've had sixteen years I never thought I would have. I can honestly say that the quality of life I've had in these years far surpasses the quality of life I had before.' Her voice became shaky. Then as she spoke again the words were slow, quiet and deliberate. 'When you've had an encounter with the living God, your life is never the same because you get things into perspective.'

She sat down, her face glowing. The congregation began to sing the well-loved words of a carol. She turned and smiled at Noel. He grinned back. *She's a wonderful speaker*, he thought. She had such an understanding of spiritual life. What a lovely talk she had given. It was the crowning moment of the highlight year. He sat back on his chair and relaxed.

Part Two

The Siege of Strangeways

Our God of the past. Eleven years have done great and mighty things at the prison. We rejoice in that. Satan has tried to destroy eleven years of faithful ministry, but Jesus has promised, 'I will build my church and the gates of hell shall not prevail against it.'

Our God of the present. God has noted our tears, our questioning, and our brokenness. And his love is healing us by reminding us of his promise, 'Don't struggle, but be still and know that I am God.'

So wrote Norma in the front of the new Bible she gave to Noel in May 1990 to replace the one ruined by fire and water in the burned-out Strangeways chapel.

8

Passion Sunday
1st April 1990

Noel shook his head as he waited to collect the men
who wanted to come to one of the Lenten Series meetings. Usually it was a simple job for the prison officer
in the centre box to read the list and send for the
prisoners. He could see clearly down all the wings.
But at the beginning of March twenty tons of scaffolding had been erected in the centre so that redecorating
could take place. Noel looked at the scaffolding. He
had seen the inmates looking at it too, especially when
the men erecting it had been clambering up and down it
like monkeys. He had heard one or two daring each
other to climb it. The scaffolding blocked visibility for
the officer on duty in the centre box. The planks made
the third landing dark too, and lights had been put
underneath to enable the officer to see more clearly.
Somehow tempers became frayed when the lads were
gathering to be taken to different classes and the
chapel. It caused tension, which later dissipated as
the classes got underway.

Things did not feel quite right in the prison either.
Ever since January there had been a build-up of lifers—
men who had been given a life sentence and transferred
from other prisons to Strangeways; men who had been

given no date for release and therefore no reason *not* to be rebellious. Their bad tempers were the cause of some confrontation. A lot of staff began talking about their concern. Pressure was mounting, not least because over-crowding was becoming an issue again. Prisoners were 'banged-up' for long hours. They only had buckets in the cells. Often the stench was appalling. The tiny cell windows had wire over them. Conditions inside the cells were not good. Slopping out was not pleasant.

On Mothering Sunday Norma came in and spoke at the main chapel service. As she left she nudged Noel. He looked at her. 'Noel,' she glanced round and shrugged helplessly. 'Noel, there's something wrong in the church.'

'What do you mean?'

She closed her eyes momentarily and then said, 'The atmosphere, it's . . . not like before. Well, it's just not there any more. And the lads didn't respond the way they've normally done in the past.'

Noel nodded. 'There's a lot of pressure at the moment,' he said. 'Maybe you've picked that up.'

In spite of Norma's words God blessed that service and a number of men asked for counselling at the end. During the following week some committed their lives to Christ. Yet, even so, as the week progressed Norma still felt that something was wrong.

On Saturday 31st March men were brought into the chapel as usual to see a film. After it was over they remained seated. Almost immediately one officer realised that this was a planned refusal to leave. Some even charged the gates at the back of the chapel. And there was trouble as the staff endeavoured to get them back onto the wings.

Noel arrived at the prison at 7.10am on the Sunday morning of 1st April. As he came into the prison to give out his list for the 8.30am communion service, he was met by one of the Governors who said, 'Noel, there are rumours that we could have trouble this morning.'

Noel said, 'Well, what do you suggest?' They both knew that Strangeways lived with rumours. There were always rumours that there was going to be trouble.

The Governor replied, 'Well, we'll put some extra staff into the chapel for the services.'

'Right,' said Noel. 'Thanks for letting me know.'

All was well at the 8.30am communion service. In fact Noel felt surprised by how well the men behaved and how quiet they were. He knew they were all believers, and it had been a lovely service. As the men left one came up to Noel and without looking at him said in a low voice, 'I'm not coming to the 10.15—there's rumours of trouble.' And then he slipped away. Noel frowned.

At 9.00am he and the Roman Catholic priest, Father Smith, exchanged chapels and each took a service. Noel was in the Roman Catholic chapel for the service for the remand prisoners, and Father Smith was in the main chapel leading a service for the Roman Catholic prisoners. Both services went well and were trouble free.

Then Noel came from the chapel in the Remand Wing back to the main prison to take the 10.15am service for the convicted prisoners. Before it began he went to the back as the men were being brought in and spoke to the senior officer in charge. 'I'm concerned because there are rumours of trouble today. One of the Governors met me this morning and told me, and one of the lads mentioned it too after communion.'

'We think everything should be all right,' replied the senior officer. 'We've got the extra staff in.'

'OK,' said Noel, and went down to the front again.

As Noel waited for the 300 or so men to be brought in from the back, and the young offenders from the side, he noticed that when the Category A prisoners (those who had committed very serious crimes) were brought in, along with those from the Segregation Unit, a lot of men turned round to stare at them. There was tension in the air, but Noel shrugged it off and announced the first hymn. It was hard to put his finger on what was wrong, but Noel recognised that there was an atmosphere, a pressure, in the service. When the hymn before the sermon was announced ten prisoners refused to stand. Noel walked rapidly over to them. 'Come on, lads,' he said. 'Show some respect in God's house. When we come into his house we stand to sing.' At this most pulled themselves to their feet. A couple remained seated. Noel turned round and marched back. He glanced at Ian Ferguson, the Church Army captain who was leading the service with him. The singing continued. Then the visiting speaker gave a brief sermon. This was received well, with some clapping.

Finally, Noel moved to give out the last hymn and opened his mouth to say, 'When I Survey the Wondrous Cross.' All at once a young man shot down the centre aisle, straight to the choir's microphone, and grabbed it. 'We've heard this morning how God is able to deal with the hardness of men's hearts,' he shouted at the top of his voice. 'I want to talk to you about the brutality of prison officers.' A string of obscenities poured from his mouth. His face and neck were covered with small beads of perspiration. He began to scream into the microphone. Noel ran forward and wrestled the microphone back from him. He pulled it with such force that he banged it into his own eye, which later swelled up, bruised and painful. The young man immediately quietened. Noel grabbed the opportunity to speak to the inmates through the microphone.

They had all risen to their feet. A wave of restless energy crackled round them.

'All right, lads,' he cried. 'I know many of you do not want to be involved in a fracas. Sit down and we'll get you out as soon as possible. I know you don't want trouble and we'll get you back to the cells as quickly as we can.'

About three-quarters of the prisoners then sat down. One officer began to try and usher the young offenders out down a side passage.

As Noel kept talking, a Category A prisoner raced down from the back of the chapel, closely followed by another inmate who was brandishing two sticks. They tore off after the young offenders' officer and knocked him down the stairs in the passage. 'Right, lads!' a prisoner shouted. 'Let's get them now!'

The young man who had initially grabbed Noel's microphone had gone very still and quiet as he saw what was going on, but now he was suddenly galvanised into life again. He tore away from Noel's side and rushed towards an officer who had come in from the vestry to stand with Noel as he tried to calm down the men over the microphone. The young man hit the officer on the head and shoulder in one great swipe. The officer fell unconscious to the ground.

Suddenly all the prisoners were on their feet. Shouting filled the chapel. Fists waved. Feet banged the floor. *That's it*, thought Noel. *The balloon's gone up*. The orderly rows of seated prisoners disappeared as men milled, shoved and yelled. Some inmates rushed over to where the officer was lying on the floor. They began to kick him. 'No!' cried Noel. 'They're not going to put the boot in!' He rushed straight for the booted, kicking group. With a force he didn't know he possessed, he pushed and knocked some of them out of the way.

All around the chapel men were pulling out homemade hoods that had been concealed under their clothing, and thrusting their heads into them. Some drew out sticks or chair legs. One picked up a clergy chair and brandished it as a weapon. Another began to rip out a front pew. Windows smashed. Many prisoners were panic-stricken, desperate to get out and not be involved. But doors were locked. They could not escape.

'Help me, lads!' shouted Noel to the group of ten or so who were sitting, shocked, in the choir. Some of these choir lads raced towards Noel, and between them all, they pulled the officer out from under the boots and away out of the chapel. Then, in a flash, the first young man appeared at Noel's side, ran down alongside the officer, snatched at his keychain and pulled it from him. He turned and ran up the left side of the chapel, shouting, 'I've got the keys!'

This is trouble, thought Noel. He gave chase after the man with the keys, running up the stairs in the chapel. But halfway up a young lad confronted him, waving a fire extinguisher above his head. Without stopping to think, Noel shouted, 'Drop it! Immediately!' Much to Noel's surprise he dropped it at once. By then it was too late to grab the keys back. The young man clutching them was already at the back of the chapel, mingling with the gang of prisoners. The noise was deafening. There was violent movement everywhere.

Ian Ferguson found himself leading about sixty prisoners out to safety. 'Please let us out,' they pleaded. 'Let us out.' He was able to get them away to a place of safety, where each was accounted for.

Noel turned and found a crowd of young inmates from the choir following him. They surrounded him, their faces furrowed.

'Don't go up there, Noel. We don't want you to get hurt.'

'Noel, we don't want you to go to the back.'

'We don't want anything to happen to you.'

'Come on, let's get out of here. Let's get out to the vestry.'

'We want to get out as well.'

So they surrounded him and led him back down again.

It was only later that Noel realised he must have been in shock by then, as he could not recollect what was happening for a few minutes. Somehow the vestry door was open. Later one of the lads from the choir told Noel that the young man who had grabbed the keys had come back down again and unlocked the vestry door to let them out. But as things were happening Noel had no conscious memory of it.

Once inside the vestry the ten or so prisoners built a barricade against the door, using a table and chairs from in there. They were all agitated and upset and it took Noel about twenty minutes to calm them down. He put his hand in his pocket and it closed over his own bunch of keys. *Strange*, he thought. *I'd forgotten I had them in all the uproar. Funny that the vestry door had been open.* As he looked round the choir lads it struck him with some force that he was one among ten prisoners, and that he had the keys. 'Let me take a list of your names,' he said. 'And then I'll vouch for you that you wanted nothing to do with all this. I *know* I know you all, but I think I'd better write a list.'

'I were panic-stricken back there,' said one of the men. 'I were looking round and wondering, "Where can I go? We're all locked in."'

'Yes,' said another, 'I was scared to death. We don't want to get in with that Category A mob.'

After a few minutes Noel decided to go for help. 'You stay here,' he said. 'I'll go down to the office and see if I can get help.'

There was a banging and a thumping overhead and several of the men ducked and then looked up rather fearfully.

'It must be them. They've got to the roof!'

'Like that lad last Monday who had to be talked down.'

Noel started. It was true that a lad had gone up that day. He had forgotten that.

'Look,' said Noel, 'I'll have to lock you in, but I'll be back as soon as I can. You are at least safe here.'

A crash was heard, followed by another, and another. 'Slates!'

'Started on that game, have they? Chucking slates.'

The noises outside grew louder and the thumping more intense. 'I'll *have* to go,' said Noel. 'We need help.'

He tried his key in the gate leading to his office and it turned. Once there he phoned the security officer, who assured Noel he would get the men out as soon as possible. Noel grabbed some packets of biscuits from his cupboard and ran back to the vestry. 'Here you are, lads,' he said. 'It's long past your dinner-time.' They looked relieved and helped themselves.

It was three-quarters of an hour before Security were able to get through to reach them and lead them away to the Visiting Room, where everyone trying to get out had gathered. The room was full of prisoners and staff.

Suddenly Noel saw Ian Ferguson coming towards him. 'Noel, where've you been? We couldn't work out where you were.' Ian hugged Noel and the tears trickled down his face. 'We've been so worried. No one knew where you were, because you were unaccounted for. I was so worried.'

Noel took his arm. 'Are *you* all right?'

'Mmm. I got a group of about sixty out. The organist helped me.' Ian shook his head. 'What an experience.'

'They're chucking slates now,' said Noel. 'They are on the roof.'

Ian said, 'It's fire that worries me.'

They looked round the crowded room. 'None of them have eaten. It's going to be some job to look after this lot.'

'Yes,' said Ian. 'Quite a few prisoners have been withdrawn from the main prison building now. And most staff have been withdrawn to the gate.'

'Are they safe?' Noel asked, thinking of the slates.

Ian shrugged.

Someone tapped Noel on the shoulder. 'The Governor wants to see you straight away,' he said. 'He's in Security.' Noel looked at his watch. It was 1.00pm. He spent some time trying to explain to the Governor and the security team what had happened in the chapel that morning. It was gruelling to have to go over it—the first of many, many times he was to relive that event of Passion Sunday morning, April Fools' Day 1990.

Eventually the Governor asked him to go to the Remand Visits Area to help the Principal Officer cope with about eighty inmates from the hospital and the kitchen. 'Some of those lads have mental problems, Noel. Some are very ill. Can you go and give some help and comfort to them?'

Noel nodded. 'Of course I will.' He glanced out of the window and the Governor followed his gaze. Both men stood in silence and watched. Officers in riot helmets were holding up perspex shields to make a corridor from the Visiting Room to the main gate. Other shields were held on top to offer protection as prisoners and staff from the Visiting Room began to run the gauntlet to get away.

Up on the roof pranced a mob of prisoners. Many

wore bags over their heads with slits cut for eyes and mouths. Fists waved. Voices screamed. Tiles were hurled. Other missiles rained down from the roof. The shields were battered as men tried to get out of the way. Some staff and inmates had been injured on the wings. Friends and colleagues helped the injured to safety. A further shower of slates, stones and bricks clattered down. *What a lot of courage among the staff out there*, thought Noel as he saw a brick bounce off a prison officer's back as he hung onto his shield, covering two inmates, one of whom was limping. He was to reflect afterwards that he had seen heroism and wonderful professionalism among the staff that day. He also saw bravery among the prisoners.

By the end of the day the majority of the men had surrendered and been bussed away to other prisons. Of the men in the chapel, Noel was sure that about three-quarters had been taken by surprise; they had been so quick to sit down when he asked them to.

The opportunity of escape into Manchester must have been uppermost in some inmates' minds that day. What a security nightmare that would have been, with escapees all over the city. Yet amazingly not one prisoner escaped. All were accounted for. It amazed Noel afterwards that prisoners stood outside the prison waiting for buses to take them to other prisons or police cells, apparently quite content to abide by the law. Prisoners still inside were ringing up the switchboard from all parts of the main prison asking to be taken out, anxious not to be involved.

Noel looked at the Governor. 'I'll get over to Remand Visits and help the Principal Officer.' And off he went.

9

'All My Work Is Ruined'

At home Norma was lying in bed early in the morning, awake, and knowing Noel had already set off for his usual Sunday morning services at the prison. She stretched and then gave herself over to reflection. Today was 1st April, Becky's seventeenth birthday. Norma looked back over all those years with thankfulness. 'Thank you, Lord,' she breathed, 'for these seventeen years.' She remembered when Becky was a few months old, when she had been diagnosed as having cancer. She had wondered if she would ever live to see Becky grow up. *And I have*, she thought. *She is seventeen, beautiful and intelligent, and like Susan and Helen, very precious.* She paused. 'Thank you, God, for the blessing of life.'

Everything in the room seemed to quieten. Norma herself lay still. She felt her hands by her side. She knew her body through and through. It had served her well all these years. She lay on for a few moments, wondering. No, she thought, *not today. This day is to be a happy day, a birthday celebration for Becky's special day.*

Later Susan, who was off duty, was taking charge of lunch preparation. Norma knew Noel would be home soon for the birthday celebration. Helen was working at college towards her finals, but would no doubt be on the phone sooner or later. Becky was upstairs. Norma could hear the murmur of the radio on in the kitchen beneath the clatter of dishes. She sniffed. The roast smelled good too.

'Mum!'

Norma started.

'Mum! Quick!'

She ran into the kitchen where Susan was standing staring at the radio. 'It's a newsflash, Mum.'

' . . . a riot at Strangeways Prison, which began in the chapel . . . ' said the announcer.

They stared at each other. 'Oh no!' said Norma. 'What about Noel? What on earth has happened?'

They rushed into the front room and switched the TV on. After a few moments the news was broadcast and the familiar façade of Strangeways came into view.

'Hostages may have been taken. Hundreds of inmates are on the rampage. Wild and senseless destruction is taking place. Numbers may be dead. It started in the chapel . . . '

Norma and Susan clasped each other's hands. The dinner was forgotten. Norma stumbled to the phone. A few days later she was to write in the journal she began during this momentous year in their lives:

I rang the prison—no calls were getting through. I rang my Christian friends and asked if they would start praying for the situation. They assured me that they would.

Where was Noel? Susan rang round the local casualty departments, but he wasn't there.

The phone rang—it was the Methodist chaplain, Peter Went, asking if Noel had got out. 'I don't know,' was my reply. Peter told me, 'It was awful in there—chaos reigned.' He was sure Noel was all right, but it sounded hollow assurance. Father Peter

Smith rang, the Roman Catholic chaplain. 'Did Noel get out?' My answer was the same.

That afternoon the phone rang dozens of times with Christians assuring us of their love and prayers, but perhaps what meant more to me were the twenty or so calls from ex-inmates asking after Noel and assuring me, 'No one will hurt Noel.' I knew deep down that physically he would be fine, but emotionally he would be devastated. His prison; his chapel; his men; his friends; his colleagues. All the trust he had in them; all the long hard days he had worked for his Lord; the lives that had been changed by the power of God; the blessing God had poured on his ministry . . . why this? My Noel who has worked with the outcasts of society for more than twenty years and still managed to keep his naïve faith in human nature. What would this do to him?

I was never more aware of the prayers of God's people than I was that day. Each report on TV painted such an awful picture of sin and destruction. I was reminded by the Holy Spirit of the promise of God: 'Where sin abounds, grace does much more abound.'

The phone rang endlessly. I kept hoping it would be Noel, but still no word. I had calls from prison officers' wives, and we tried to comfort and reassure each other.

Becky had spent much of the afternoon in her bedroom. I went to her and loved her. This sophisticated seventeen-year-old, so often cool and detached, looked at me with tears in her eyes and then wept, 'It's my birthday, and I want my dad.'

At about 6pm John Hargreaves (the Assistant Chaplain General) rang to say, 'Noel is safe. He is in the prison with about 100 inmates who wanted no part of the riot. When they can get these men out to safety, Noel will be home.' Praise God for the good news and praise God for a caring human being like John Hargreaves.

John came to our home shortly afterwards and took me to the prison officers' mess where I spoke to Noel. 'Yes, love, I'm all right, and the lads are OK, but we're very hungry—haven't eaten since breakfast.'

John came back with me to our home. We had some tea and prayed together.

Mark Smith, our young curate, came soon after this. He was as bemused as we were at all the news. Mark didn't say much, but he just stayed with us, and his being there was a comfort.

Back at Strangeways Noel set himself to comforting the sick and disturbed prisoners in the Remand Visits section. Many were angry, many worried and tense. He became aware that he was very hungry, as the inmates were. But no one had, as yet, been able to get any food to them. In his concern and shock it did not occur to Noel that the riot would be reported on television and that Norma would find out about it and be desperately worried. Later he was to write:

I suppose at that time I didn't think of the fact that this was going out on television and radio. I didn't realise that Norma would be worrying herself sick. And it wasn't until late in the afternoon when all the lads who were in the Remand Visits were being taken out that John Hargreaves, the Assistant Chaplain General, arrived and said to me, 'Norma's worried about you,' and I was led down to the Security Office where I was able to get onto the telephone, ring Norma, and let her know that I was all right. I couldn't get away because there were so many things happening.

That night at 9.30pm, as the Governor said to me, 'It's time you were going home,' I realised I hadn't eaten since breakfast-time and I was hungry. Peter Wilkinson supported me as I got to the gate. I came out and it was dark in Southall Street. I'd left my old car over on the rough ground at the far side. It was always a quiet place over there, but that night, as I made my way across the road, suddenly I was surrounded by lights and reporters and cameras, and they wanted to know what had happened in the prison and what was happening at the moment; how it had all started. I couldn't give them very much, but they wanted answers. I spoke to them for a few moments. I didn't realise that it was going out on television—not only throughout this country, but in other parts of the world as well. In fact my brother in Canada said that there was a shot of me on Canadian television.

When I got home the house was surrounded by reporters wanting to talk. They had asked my wife for stories, and for photographs, and it was Becky's birthday. It was 1st April. And as I came in through the door, suddenly Becky came into the hall. I know she loves me, but that night she put her arms round me, and she sobbed and she sobbed, 'Oh Dad, I'm so glad you're all right.' That child was so worried about her dad, and as I tried to say to her, 'I'm all right, love. Don't be worrying,' her mum said to me, 'All day she's kept saying, "The only birthday present I want is my dad to come home. I want my dad home."'

Noel had not arrived home until 10 o'clock that night. Norma saw his face as he walked in through the front door: grey, drawn and with a black eye. He explained to her that the injury to his eye was self-inflicted in his struggle with the young man at the microphone. All the while, as they stood in the hall, Becky clung to him as if she never wanted to let go of her father again. Norma immediately ran Noel a hot bath. She had realised at once by looking at him that he was in shock. So when she offered him something to eat and he refused, she did not press any food on him.

'Come on,' she said. 'Let's get you upstairs into a nice warm bath. And then bed! I insist.' Noel allowed himself to be ushered upstairs. Bath and a bed were all he felt he could cope with. He found he could not even speak to them all much, he was so exhausted.

Norma put the answer-phone on and said, 'Now we'll get some peace.'

But at around 11pm the door-bell rang. Norma flew to open the front door only to be confronted by a reporter from the national press. 'Can I just have a picture of the reunited family?' he demanded.

'No,' said Norma, her eyes glinting. 'It's far too late.'

'But it's my brief.'

'No, certainly not!' she snapped.

'I'll camp outside the house all night then!'

Norma slammed the door shut. At that moment she couldn't have cared less how he was to spend his night. Her only concern was how her Noel was ever going to get through his.

Finally she eased her way into bed and lay beside him, knowing he was awake but with his eyes closed. She longed to talk to him; to help him by letting him share the agonies and frustrations of the day with her. But he lay quite still and unrelaxed, like a stranger. *I've shared his life for twenty-six years*, she thought, *and now in the hour of his greatest need he is withdrawn and uncommunicative*. She bit her lip and turned over.

It would be best, she knew both as a wife and an experienced nurse, to let him take his own time to recover sufficiently to be able to talk to her. But it hurt even so, and it was a long time before she slept.

Noel himself lay awake all night, longing for sleep; but sleep would not come. He found he could not speak about the experience yet—even to Norma. It was as if he were still steeling himself for further shocks. If he did let the barricades down, he did not know if there would be any Noel Proctor left to do anything at all in this world. As he lay quite rigid in their bed, he found the events of the day replayed through his mind. Over and over he saw the young man running towards him, snatching the microphone. He saw the officer unconscious on the floor, with a jeering crowd 'booting' him. He saw the chapel, his chapel, being wrecked and destroyed. He remembered with a shudder that the cross up on the chapel roof had been hurled down to the yard below. And he had lost his Bible, which Norma had given him on their twenty-third Wedding Anniversary.

Then the events of his past life began to replay themselves in his mind interminably, as his over-active imagination refused to relax. He remembered 1973 when he felt as if something had died within him: too late to see his father before he died, his mother's death, Norma's miscarriage and their lost baby, Norma's cancer. It had all been so hard, so very, very hard, to search for and rediscover faith. He shifted in the bed, aware now that Norma was asleep at last. It was true that in the past seventeen years they *had* rediscovered their faith in Jesus Christ and his power. Well, he had to admit to himself, *he* had. Norma's had never foundered in the way his had done.

But now? He tried to blank out his thoughts, and found it was no good. After eleven years of work at

Strangeways Prison, during which he and the team had seen many lives touched and transformed by the power of the gospel, everything was falling in around him. The great wall of faith and work he had built up was collapsing in a shower of slates, violence and obscenities. Why had it all happened? Was it his fault? Had he done anything wrong and was there anything he could have done to stop it? He had taken the mike from the lad who had grabbed it that morning. He had talked the lads down. He had encouraged them to sit down again in their seats. He had felt completely alone at the time but that he was needed to be there. And then when the prisoner ran down the aisle and attacked an officer, somehow he knew that was it and there was no way he could stop this thing getting completely out of hand.

By the time it was growing light on Monday 2nd April Noel was up. 'I'll have to go in, Norma,' he said on his way out. 'I'm sorry.' She nodded and kept calm. He kissed her goodbye.

Suddenly she grabbed his arm. 'I'll bet those reporters are still out there waiting for you.' She ran and peeped through the bedroom curtains. 'Yes,' she called. 'They are. There's two carloads of them outside.' She thought for a moment and then said, 'Can you get out at the back?'

Momentarily the ghost of a smile hovered on his face. 'You bet I can,' he said. He slipped out of the back door and through into the garage before any of the reporters were aware of the fact. Then he was out and away down the road before they managed to follow him. Becky did not fare so well. As she left the house to go to school, she found herself surrounded by them and their insistent questions. It took her some time to get away.

As Noel drove towards Manchester he was surprised to find all the traffic stopped and diverted by the police.

He managed to get through and made his way towards the main gate. As he did, the first thing to hit him was the noise of shouting and screaming from the prisoners on the roof. He rounded a corner and looked up at the bright April sky. There on the roof were groups of men. Most wore gags or bags on their heads. Some wore officers' peaked caps. They pranced, screamed and jeered. Fists waved. Slates hailed down. Many rafters were showing. Some prisoners were hunched astride the apex of the chapel roof; some sat nearer the parapets for security. Torsoes were bared. Verbal abuse hurled down, along with the rain of bricks and missiles. It was an ugly and dangerous sight. One had a megaphone and was shouting. After a moment, Noel realised that the prisoners were playing to the gallery of the press gathered outside in Southall Street.

It makes me sick, he thought and his hands clenched. A wave of anger shot over him—fury that the inmates were doing this. And underneath the anger was an emptiness. After all the blessing of the past years and months, all the hard work, seeing all the lives touched and changed by the power of God, this was happening. Indeed, where was God in all this?

Even as he dashed into the officers' club next to the main gate, slates continued to hurl down. There were torrents of hatred and abuse. And there was always the threat of fire, of an inferno developing. Someone gave Noel a cup of tea. As he drank it he looked around at the faces of staff in there and saw the looks of despair, anguish and hurt. It was a scene he was never to forget. Some asked how he was and he was able to chat a little.

Later on a tea-bar was set up in the mess for the twenty-five days of the siege. This became a God-sent area as everybody worked together: staff, firemen, policemen, education personnel, probation officers and others. The chaplaincy team manned the tea-bar, doing eight-hour shifts. They found they were often to play a counselling role—sometimes able to help staff families as well.

As the day progressed Martin Fielding, the Diocesan Press Officer, came to see Noel, took a statement from him and from all members of the team and handled the press on the chaplaincy's behalf. As the days went by Noel realised how helpful and supportive Martin was and he became more than grateful for his help, particularly as during those first few days the press hounded him and his family.

Towards lunchtime the Governor came to Noel and, realising he was in shock, said, 'I don't want you here today. Go on home. Get some sleep.' So Noel was persuaded to leave and was accompanied by Father Peter Wilkinson, the senior Roman Catholic chaplain, all the way home in the car. Once home they realised that Norma was on duty at Heathlands, so Peter waited with him until Noel was settled in bed. Noel and Peter knew each other well, had worked together in the past, and were like brothers to each other. 'Come on, Noel,' said Peter. 'You must get some rest.'

'Could I have done something to stop this terrible chaos?' asked Noel. 'Am I to blame?'

'No. No. No.'

'But all my work is ruined, isn't it?'

Then, even with the questioning still uppermost in his mind, Noel fell asleep at last. Peter quietly left the room.

10

'You Have Experienced Your Crucifixion'

Back at the prison smoke was drifting out of some of the cell windows, settling in a grey-yellow cloud above the building. A police helicopter hovered overhead, monitoring the whole situation. The rioters on the roof had tried raising clenched fists at it and hurling bricks towards it, but had given that up as pointless.

Down below, amid the noise of their jeers and sirens wailing, prisoners who wanted to get out were still running for the main gate. Officers in riot gear, helmeted with see-through visors, wielded their shields. Some ran with an injured inmate on a stretcher. Paramedics waited to put the man into an ambulance. Hospitals were standing by. Policemen were there too, truncheons in pockets or held in readiness. The Prison Officers' Association Branch Chairman gave a brief interview to the press, in which he indicated that he was saying very little about what was happening. 'The prisoners may be listening in now,' he explained. 'They will have radios and will be following everything.'

By the evening only 119 inmates were unaccounted for. Some of these had used the prison switchboard to telephone out to a local newspaper with their demands: these centred around better conditions inside the prison, better conditions for visitors when they came, and improvements for remand prisoners.

There were confused eye-witness accounts from escaping prisoners, who spoke of wings blackened by fire; cell doors wrenched off their hinges, bed frames thrown into the wells between the landings which were piled up with mattresses, chairs, buckets and a mass of debris. Planks of wood had been ripped out, and there were holes in the walls where bricks had been torn out. Graffiti was painted on the dirtied grey walls in a jumble of black and grey capital letters. By evening, part of the building was ablaze, and the night sky was lit up by flames and smoke. The fire could be seen raging inside the prison through the cell windows, which glowed red against the silhouetted building.

It became known that the Governor had made contingency plans to storm the prison, using nearly 400 officers to regain control. However, the Deputy Director of the Prison Service decided this could run the risk of injury or even death to some officers, as the situation was so volatile. He decided that the plan to storm the jail should not go ahead. So began the twenty-five-day siege of Strangeways. In retrospect, it was seen that this was the worst riot in the history of the British Prison Service. One prisoner died in hospital afterwards from natural causes. One officer, Wally Scott, died on 5th April in Bury Hospital as a result of a heart attack on the Sunday night. Forty-seven prisoners were injured over all and 147 police and staff were injured too. Many staff suffered afterwards from stress and post-traumatic shock, which took a long time for full recovery. Many staff were sent on detached duty to prisons all over the country, which meant they were separated from family and friends. Prisoners too were sent all over England. As a result they too were not able to see family. Those involved with the chaplaincy and meetings were bussed away along with all the others, and this was not easy for them.

On 5th April the Home Secretary, David Wadding-ton, announced a judicial enquiry, to be headed by Lord Justice Woolf. This was to become a turning point for all involved in the British Penal System: the Government, staff, inmates, the Prison Service, chaplaincy teams, all other professionals and lay visitors involved in prisons, and for those concerned with penal reform and the rehabilitation of offenders.

By 1.30pm on the afternoon of Monday 2nd April Norma was off duty at Heathlands Nursing Home where she worked as a Sister, and arrived home. She checked on Noel and found him sleeping peacefully at last and ran downstairs again. Moments later she saw Captain Ian Ferguson coming up the steps to the front door. She later wrote:

Ian, bless him, Noel's constant colleague in all his years at Strangeways. They were like brothers; not physically, for Ian's hefty fifteen stone was like Goliath to Noel's ten stone, but spiritually they were brothers in Christ.

Ian embraced Susan and me and we had a coffee together. I said, 'How was it, Ian?' and the emotional dam burst its banks. Ian cried and cried.

'Oh, Norma, Noel went into the middle of the rioters trying to calm them and I thought they would kill him. One man lifted a fire extinguisher to bring it down on Noel, and I just thought that was it.'

Noel was garrisoned by prayer and the hosts of God were protecting him. I knew this without a doubt.

I asked Noel about this incident much later and he

said, 'Yes, I told the lad to drop the extinguisher, and he did. I wasn't brave, Norma. I just had no sense of danger in the chapel.' Then he witnessed the attack on the prison officer, and also the courage of the prisoners who got him to safety.

During those weeks Noel spoke only of the wonderful professionalism of the Strangeways officers, and found in the weeks following the riot that the bond between chaplain and officers was strengthened.

We received hundreds of phone calls of love and reassurance. By this time we had received about 800 letters and cards from Christians and non-Christians. One that moved me to tears was from the Jewish Rabbi at the prison, who spoke of his love and respect for Noel and assured us of his prayers.

Noel threw himself into the shift rota, working round the clock with the chaplaincy team. The Governor described the riot as 'an explosion of evil' and we realised that because God's blessing had rested on Strangeways, Satan had attacked and tried to destroy it.

Jesus said, 'I will build my church and the gates of hell will not prevail against it.'

Still no tears from Noel; still withdrawn; still spiritually bruised and broken. Why, Lord?

Norma put down her pen, knowing that she would have to give Noel time before he would be able to talk about this experience and relate to her again. She bit her lip and found herself praying for the courage to carry on while he remained so locked up in himself.

Noel continued to work long hours at the prison. Everyone there began to be affected by feelings of tension, anxiety, fear and rejection. His own thoughts were confused and muddled. Everyone was hurt deeply, both emotionally and spiritually. Those in the chaplaincy team were no exception, but through it all they tried to support each other. All the letters and phone calls and prayer built up a solid wall of support, and this meant a great deal to Noel. He said later that they had no contingency plans for what to do as chaplains, yet the Governor wanted them to be involved, and so in the days that followed sometimes they got very little sleep.

The chaplaincy as a team looked after the tea-bar in the Officers' Club and went out to visit prisoners in police cells, not only in Manchester but on the outskirts of Manchester too. They went to the hospital to see those who had been hurt. When Wally Scott had his heart attack on the night of Sunday 1st April, Noel visited him in hospital and went on afterwards to see his wife.

The chaplains visited the homes of staff too. The Bishop of Manchester allowed the church hall at St Clements near Waterloo Road to be used for the families of prisoners who were on the roof; families who were worried about what was happening to some of their loved ones who were inside. And so it became a meeting place where the chaplains went each day to see the families there, to try to reassure them, to try to give them comfort. Each morning the chaplaincy team would meet in the Visitors' Centre in Caernarvon Street, which had now become the place of meeting for all the different organisations; for probation; for the chaplaincy; for all those who were involved in any way; for staff who needed comfort and counsel. The Bishop of Manchester came many mornings to pray with them, and then Garth Rogers, the Methodist chaplain, took over the job of speaking to the media, because he realised that it was too much for Noel. And

Noel found this a tremendous help throughout the whole period.

After the first few days they decided that they would work on an eight-hour shift each, so that a chaplain would be there round the clock. Noel often found himself walking round the prison at 2 o'clock in the morning, going down to the Officers' Mess where he could get something to eat, to give to the firemen, police or staff who were on standby; endeavouring to help, and to encourage them.

On Tuesday 3rd April Noel drove down early to the prison so that he could help man the tea-bar. But when he arrived he was asked to help in the negotiations with and counselling of some thirteen lads who wanted to come down from the roof. As he was standing waiting to go and talk to them he realised he could hear shouting from the roof. He stepped back and looked up. Nearby was a fireman with a hose trained onto the smouldering cells. Suddenly Noel shouted, 'Lend me your hose!'

The fireman looked at him, startled. 'What for?'

Noel cried, 'These blackguards!'

The fireman followed his gaze and the two of them watched helplessly as the rioters paraded up and down in vestments they had stolen from the chapel. Abuse floated down on the breeze from the roof.

'Give me that hose, I say!' shouted Noel. 'I'm going to baptise them! I'll not only baptise them, I'll wash them off the roof! I'll get them off the roof if it's the last thing I do!'

The fireman kept his hose firmly trained onto the flames and smoke that were flaring out of the cell windows. 'I never thought I'd hear a chaplain say that,' he said and shook his head.

Noel clenched his fists. 'But I'm so angry!' he cried.

Yet the great surge of anger was soon to give way to

the old feeling of emptiness inside him. He knew perfectly well that hoses were never used in such a way. As he trailed slowly back to the barricade in order to help with negotiating, he realised suddenly how tired he was; he was not thinking straight. As he made his way to the barricade and surrender point on F Wing, the full force of many negatives struck him: fear, horror, destruction—all were happening in a place where people had worked and given of themselves for years.

This particular day the thirteen inmates surrendered. Members of the Board of Visitors, chaplains, doctors and prison officers were all involved in the negotiations and in seeing the men as they came down. Over the twenty-five days of the siege Noel had witnessed no assaults on prisoners by any staff. There were, however, times when a few hard-core prisoners had come and chased away other prisoners from the barricades, who had wanted to get out.

Noel decided to go home for lunch and as he opened his front door he heard voices. He stepped into the front room and saw Norma sitting talking to Sister Dominic.

'Hello there,' he said.

Sister Mary Dominic lived at the convent on the Bury New Road. She was a little, elderly Roman Catholic nun, who often came in to the prison to take classes and pray in the prayer groups. On the table was a bouquet of flowers and Noel guessed she had brought them for Norma. He opened his mouth to say something, but Sister Dominic looked at him. She drew herself to her feet and embraced him.

'Oh, Noel,' she said in her Southern Irish accent. 'Noel. This is Passion Week and like our Lord, you feel alone. The men you have trusted have left you. Noel, you have experienced your crucifixion. You've had your tragedy, you've had your heartaches, you've had your tears. Your work seems to have fallen in around you. Like the Master as he saw his disciples scattered, you've seen your congregation scattered. Your flock has gone to prisons all over the country. Oh yes,' she said, 'you have been crucified, but God is going to give you a glorious resurrection. A resurrection that is far greater than you can ever imagine. Easter is ahead and you will know new life in Christ. New beginnings, a whole new ministry.'

With this word of discernment she stopped. Noel stared at her helplessly and burst into tears. A little while later he drove her back to the convent. Afterwards, when he came back out of the convent, he sat in his car and simply sobbed.

Later he realised that this was the turning point. He said:

I suppose it was then that I began to experience something of God's healing power in my life. Up until then I was in shock. I was in anger. I was in hurt. Now, as the tears flowed and as I sobbed, I could feel the love of God beginning to flow into my life. People prayed for me. People loved me. Even though the hurt was so great. In the days that followed I got phone call after phone call. On that Sunday when the tragedy happened, Norma said that the phone never stopped ringing. Many of the callers were ex-prisoners who reassured her and said, 'Nothing'll happen to Noel. They all love him.' She was frightened and those ex-prisoners reassured her.

And in the weeks that followed we received over a thousand letters from many people all over the country, and all over the world, assuring us of prayer, assuring us of God's love, saying that God had scattered the Christians who were in Strangeways Prison in order to bring blessing to others. And how true this was. We heard so many stories from different parts of the country, where prisoners had been witnessing to the power of Jesus Christ in their lives. But how it hurt. It hurt to think that the work that had been going on in Strangeways over those years had suddenly disintegrated. It was no longer happening. Oh it hurt, and the tears flowed.

Up until this point Noel had been unable to talk about his experience in the chapel. He could not share it with anyone. Norma grew in her understanding of this and wrote in her journal about Sister Dominic's visit:

So time passed and Noel went through varying changes. No public speaking, no TV or radio interviews. No newspaper reporter could entice him to agree to an interview. The healing process was beginning and the doubts, fears and suffering—yes and bitterness—were slowly fading; but today look into Noel's heart and note the scars left from the agony. Search his mind and you will find many of his questions unanswered. He is coping in God's strength and will know his Easter in God's timing.

11

Seeing Through a Darkened Glass

One morning shortly after Sister Dominic's visit, and when Norma was off duty, she took out her journal and began to write. The house was very quiet and her pen flew across the page. Every now and again she paused, thought and wrote again. After an hour or so she stopped and put her pen down. She stared unseeingly out of the window. She looked around the room in the house which she and Noel had built up together. Then, slowly, she picked up the journal and read what she had written. She had begun with the day of the riot—Becky's birthday:

Sunday morning, 7.00am. Noel was already on his way to the prison. At home I was still in bed, but awake. Today was Sunday, but it was also Becky's seventeenth birthday. I looked back over those years with thankfulness to God, remembering when she was just months old and I was diagnosed as having cancer. I wondered if I would ever see her grown up. Now she is seventeen, beautiful, intelligent and like Susan and Helen very, very precious.

Thank you, God, for the blessing of life.

I have known for some months that I now have a secondary spread of the cancer. I knew when Noel went to Withington Hospital to have a rodent ulcer removed from his face. I couldn't tell him how I was when he needed me, and with God's help I would be there with him.

Christmas came and I thought that perhaps it was my last with the family. I could not feel depressed. God was in control of our lives and I knew only peace.

1990: This year Susan had her midwifery finals, Helen her degree finals and last teaching practice, and Becky her first year 'A' level exams.

The family come first, although watching the changes in my body I know there is no recession of the cancer. My strength and my peace I find daily in the assurance of Christ's love for me, and my faith in him is steadfast.

1st April was to be a happy day. Helen was working at college towards her finals, but Susan was off duty, and so I knew that when Noel came home to lunch we would celebrate Becky's special day.

Susan was taking charge of lunch preparations and the radio was on. The programme was interrupted to announce that there had been a riot at Strangeways. It had started in the chapel. We stood in disbelief. It couldn't be true—not the chapel!

There. It was written now and out in the open. Her cancer had come back after all those years. And she knew she could not tell Noel and the girls just yet. All her married life she had wanted to protect him and the girls from the knocks of the world. *Just a little while longer*, she thought, *and then I'll tell him*. She had in fact written him a letter explaining all about it, but the days had passed by and still she had not found the right moment to give it to him. Then, with the eruption of the riot, and his shocked response to it, she knew she could not devastate him further by telling him. It was

secret she was going to have to have the courage to keep
for a little while longer. She leaned back in her seat,
tired and unwilling to admit it. She knew she ought to
be filled with fear for her future, but a wonderful and
supernatural peace had held her all along. This peace
was holding her, she knew. And it would continue to
hold her.

The phone rang. As she picked it up she heard Noel's
voice. He sounded tired. 'Wally Scott's died, love. You
know, the officer who had the heart attack on Sunday
night after he'd insisted on staying to help at the
prison.'

'Oh no,' said Norma. 'His poor wife.'

'I'm going to visit her,' said Noel. 'I'll phone you.
Actually. . . ' he paused, 'they may want me to take the
funeral.'

Norma stood quietly for a moment by the phone. She
felt very sad for Wally Scott's family, but a part of her
at least was glad that at last Noel was communicating
with her again. Very slowly things were coming out:
about staff who had been hurt; about hospitals he had
visited; about wives he had tried to comfort; about
prisoners' families camped out in St Clement's Church
who needed support; about staff involved in the negotiations who were sleeping in the hospital area and who
needed reassurance; about other members of staff who
came and supported him and prayed with him. She
knew that when he was ready he would share the
deeper hurt as well. Father Peter Smith and Captain
Ian Ferguson were also welcome visitors to their home
and they too began to share some of the burden of
tension and pressure. She raised her chin a little. She
was going to play her part and continue to support
them all for as long as she could.

One morning towards the end of the first week of the
siege, Noel made his way towards the Officers' Club.

He looked up at the roof and saw some of the prisoners holding banners with messages scrawled on them. A few days before one had said, 'No Dead.' Rumours were still rife in the region about the numbers of dead. No one really knew, but horrific stories had circulated and many inmates were in hospital with the injuries they had received during the first hours of the riot, or suffering from overdoses of drugs they had stolen from the dispensary.

To counteract the noise of the prisoners shouting their demands, the police who circled the perimeter walls were playing loud music and prison officers used a screaming siren. The police helicopter was to strafe the prison building that night with an hourly beam of light. The tactic was to deprive the prisoners who were still holding out of sleep. Peaceful negotiations had seen all but thirty-eight of 1,647 prisoners now accounted for. Tactics were now to include the use of noise as a psychological weapon.

As Noel continued wearily towards the Officers' Club he saw another banner unfurled on the roof. This one read, 'We are deeply sorry for the Scott family over the loss of their father. We are human.' Noel felt too tired to respond, even with a shrug. He passed on and went inside. He knew now what the inside of the prison looked like: everything that could be torn up, or thrown down, had been done so. Landing wells were piled high with smoke-blackened debris, later soaked in water by the firefighters. The gym was wrecked. Both the chapels were completely destroyed. Much was gutted by fire. Windows were smashed. Both the chaplains' library and the Remand Centre prison library were torn apart. It had been an explosion of evil, thought Noel, for the riot had started in one chapel and moved to another. These were the only buildings to be totally destroyed. Rioting prisoners used the chalice to drink cocoa from and paraded about in vestments, mocking. One of the first things the rioters did was to push the cross off the chapel roof, smashing it onto the yard below. Noel agreed with the Governor that this was a battle between the forces of good and evil.

There was a heavy weight around his heart that seemed to have lodged itself there. He could not understand it, but he knew he felt guilty all the time. Constantly he asked himself whether there was anything he could have done on that morning of 1st April which he had not done. Was it his fault that the riot blew up out of all control? Was he to blame? Sister Dominic's words had helped him considerably, but even so he found himself questioning his faith and, more particularly, his calling. People said that he was still suffering from shock. His thoughts tended to be confused. Always he felt empty, as if nothing could reach him. And the guilt was there all the time.

After a while he came out of the Officers' Club and saw an officer he knew quite well, called Dave. Dave was collecting for Wally Scott's family and had a box in his hand. 'Come here, you idiot!' called Dave. Startled, Noel stopped. 'Just look at you! What do you think you are doing, looking so grim?' Noel permitted his tensed facial muscles to relax a little.

'You know, you're taking this thing far too seriously. This was going to happen. All right, it happened in the chapel, but it could have happened anywhere. It had nothing to do with you. It was going to happen anyway.'

Noel opened his mouth. 'Look . . .' he began, but Dave waved the collecting box at him.

'Nothing to do with you!' he repeated, emphasising each word. 'Snap out of it, Noel. If you crack up, what's going to happen to us?'

Noel looked at Dave for some moments. His words were like a welcome glass of water in a desert.

'Do you know, Dave,' he replied, 'that's the best sermon I've ever heard!'

Dave grinned and Noel went on his way, feeling somewhat lighter in spirit than he had before. Perhaps his ministry did have something to offer after all.

One of the hardest things to bear for all the staff was that a few days before the riot HM Chief Inspector of Prisons, Judge Stephen Tumin, had published a report which praised the way conditions were improving in Strangeways. Noel wrote in the first prayer letter to be sent out after the riot:

Brendan O'Friel, the Governor, and all the staff had really moved Strangeways forward, and the improvements were felt throughout the whole establishment, giving us all a sense of fulfilment and a pride in our work of rehabilitation. The Education Department was providing opportunities for inmates to improve themselves. The work in physical education had to be seen to be believed as more men and boys were being allowed to use the facilities of the various gymnasiums. The probation workers were making great strides in preparing men for release and making sure of after-care.

All the chaplains have asked 'Why?' as we have seen our work torn to pieces before our eyes and we have all been damaged and hurt in ways which take a long time to heal. At first it was a real sense of hopelessness and frustration, as the work which had taken years to build was destroyed. Then came the bitterness and anger against those who had perpetrated such evil. This was followed by the feeling of rejection and emptiness.

Oh yes, Strangeways was a tough place. It had

been called a human warehouse. We had seen so many things happening when men were packed in like sardines. And the slopping out was something of a degrading situation. But many good things had been happening since Brendan O'Friel had taken over. We were seeing more men in the workshops. We were seeing more men employed. We were seeing more people coming into the groups and classes for education and probation, and the chaplaincy. We were seeing more men taking part in the gym. And we were seeing things happening that were good, productive and positive.

Noel did take Wally Scott's funeral in North Manchester. The Chaplain General came up from London to be present at the service, as was Bishop Stanley of Manchester. This service was televised and made national news. As Noel shared his thoughts and feelings in the sermon, he said, 'During these last days we've all been hurt deeply. We have suffered two bereavements—Wally and also our prison. Every one of us has been hurt emotionally and our feelings have been confused, muddled, and we've also been hurt spiritually as the attacks of evil have bombarded us, leaving scars and wounds which will take a long time to heal. There have been those of us hurt physically. Although Wally's health had suffered over the years, I'm sure the events of Sunday 1st April increased the pressures on him. Yet, as Wally was a fighter who refused to accept defeat, he refused to go home when he was ill that night. So the message to us all, as we come to pay our respects and condolences, is to press on to victory.'

As the days of the siege went by, Noel and the other chaplains in the team slowly began to accept that all their work had indeed *not* been a waste of time and energy. The Assistant Chaplain General, John Hargreaves, spoke at the Palm Sunday service, held in the Officers' Mess and quoted Romans 8:31: 'If God be for us, who can be against us?' Slowly they regained energy and, as Noel said, 'a desire to see the phoenix arising out of the ashes; the phoenix of God's blessing, where a new prison would come with new opportunities and future blessings'.

In spite of these stirrings of hope there were still inmates parading on the roof every day, in full view of the media who appeared to be permanently camped outside. By 10th April there were fewer than twenty prisoners holding out. The Governor still used the tactic of peaceful negotiation.

Between the 13th and 18th April more inmates surrendered and three were taken to hospital with suspected food poisoning. There were now only seven hard-core prisoners left unaccounted for. On 19th April the Governor announced that all 1,647 inmates who were in the prison when the riot began were accounted for. But still the prison had not yet been recaptured. As Easter approached, many people felt they were living out a personal Holy Week. The chalice was eventually found in the ruins of the prison, quite flattened. A prisoner called 'Big Donald' said, 'Give it here,' and beat it back into a more or less recognisable shape. Noel decided to keep it safe until he could think of a use for it.

Noel was never to forget the day the Control and Restraint team said to him, 'We've taken back your chapel. Will you come and see what you can get out of it?' So the Control and Restraint team formed up, with Ian Ferguson and Noel behind them, and marched forward into the chapel, singing as they went, 'Onward Christian Soldiers.' Momentarily Noel chuckled to himself. What a sight they must look with their helmets on! But it was a sign to him that they were marching to victory. They were not marching to defeat. And afterwards the staff who had marched with them said, 'That's a picture of the future. We're not going to give in. We're going to win.'

The chuckle almost immediately died away though. It shocked the chaplains to see the devastation in the chapel. The wooden statue of Christ on the cross was smashed. The organ was completely ruined. Everything was fire-blackened and soaked in water. Every stick of furniture was torn up and thrown down anywhere. Noel simply stared at it, stunned. Later he found his Bible, completely unusable and swollen up after the soaking it had received from the firefighters. It was the one Norma had given him on their twenty-third Wedding Anniversary. Could Strangeways ever open again, he wondered? And if it did, would there ever be a new chapel?

On 25th April, with all but five prisoners now recaptured, prison officers in riot gear stormed the prison, quickly regaining control of the upper wing floors. The five fled to the roof, hurling missiles as they went. They were then faced with the choice of surrender or spending the night on the roof, surrounded by officers. By 6.00pm they decided to give themselves up. The young man who had first run down the chapel stairs on 1st April to shout his protest was the last to leave the roof. The five were taken down on a hydraulic platform, which was lorry-operated. They came down to world media coverage, punching the air, waving, clenching fists in salute and giving the thumbs-up sign. When they reached the ground they were led away. Prison officers turned to each other and shook hands, smiled and gave three cheers for the Governor.

Afterwards they made a final sweep through the prison. No bodies were found. Perhaps the sources of the rumours of sightings of dead bodies came from the sight of men who had passed out in the uproar and frenzy, overcome by drugs they had stolen from the dispensary.

Questions were asked in Parliament about the handling of the siege, and about the way media coverage may have played into the hands of the rioters. Nevertheless, the then Home Secretary, David Waddington, was adamant that any storming of the prison could have resulted in deaths and serious injury to staff and inmates alike. The facts were that in spite of prisoners parading a homemade noose on the roof to the waiting cameras below, there had been no hostages taken, no killings, and no really serious injuries. There had been no escapees, and no risk to the general public's safety. The prison officers and the Governor had done magnificent work and David Waddington was proud of them. He said that a new prison would rise from the ashes of the old. There would be a new Strangeways. That was for certain.

12

Aftermath

After the longest siege in British penal history, work
began in May to sort out the mess that was Strangeways. Refurbishment started on the remand wings
which had been relatively untouched by the rioters
and the fire. There were to be new, bigger cell windows—a prisoner would at least be able to see through
the window now, without having to stand on a chair to
do so. There was a new ventilation and heating system,
and new stainless steel cladding for the roof that would
weather to look like the old slates. Slopping out was to
be a thing of the past: each cell was to have a stainless
steel washbasin and toilet. No more of a whole wing
having to use eight toilets. It had only taken one man to
stuff his socks down the toilet for the whole place to be
flooded. Whatever a man had done, there should at
least be decency. Security and the exercise area were
also to be improved. All this would take at least a
year to complete.

In the meanwhile, the only prisoners left in Strangeways were those working in the Officers' Mess and
helpers in the kitchen. During the siege Noel had
held services in the Officers' Club. The first United
Service held in the prison was in May and took place
in the hospital waiting room. Prison visitors, helpers,
friends, chaplains, some staff and two prisoners all

came and joined in: denominational barriers no longer divided anyone. It was not a particularly comfortable place to hold a service and the toilet next door kept flushing. Yet at the end of that service one of the prisoners asked how he could become a Christian. The following Sunday fourteen prisoners came. Little by little, as the time went by, Noel saw that God was blessing again. The convent where Sister Dominic lived offered room for the Wednesday night prayer group. This idea was taken up immediately. It was truly ecumenical in spirit. Noel loved going, as did Norma. Everyone met there as brothers and sisters in Christ. People from all the denominations met together and prayed in a unity that became greater and greater.

Suddenly, after the media explosion of those twenty-five days, there was no more interest in what was happening in the prison. Those on the ground were left to pick up the pieces. Perhaps the report of the surveyors after the riot went deeper than simply being a report on the actual prison buildings. It reflected how many of the staff and inmates felt: 'Strangeways prison is structurally sound, although inside it is a mess.' Prisoners, many of whom wanted nothing to do with the riot, were sent as far away as Bridgend and Swansea Prisons. The number of marriages and relationships which fell to pieces as a result was only one aspect of the inmates' suffering. The chaplaincy received many letters from prisoners, which shared how angry and bitter some of them were with the ring-leaders of the riot.

Noel was involved in the Care Team that was formed in the prison after the riot. This was available to help staff suffering from post-traumatic or post-incident stress. Many staff were having nightmares, involuntary recurring thoughts when they relived scenes from the uproar, drinking too much or taking their troubles home with them. Team members found a great source of support in each other, as indeed did the chaplains.

One day Noel received a letter from a former inmate who had been sent to Lincoln Prison. 'I wanted to tell you that I decided to be a Christian when I was at Strangeways. I don't understand what is happening to me, but I feel Jesus has given me a new purpose in life.' One ex-inmate wrote, 'The consequences of what happened will mean that many Christian prisoners from Strangeways will have been moved to prisons all over the country and thus the Light that was in Strangeways has now been spread much further.' These were just two of the many hundreds of letters of support and encouragement received from all over the world.

Ian Ferguson, Peter Smith and Noel became involved in working with the staff in the reorganising inside the prison. One job was to pull out sheets and blankets and take them to the laundry in trucks. They found themselves laughing over this one day. 'I've found muscles I never knew I had,' cried Noel.

'Me too!' said Ian with feeling.

'I'm surprised to see you lot doing a job like that,' said a voice from behind them. Noel turned round and saw a prison officer watching them quizzically.

'Oh yes,' laughed Peter. 'We know what's good for us.'

Soon they were to put on dungarees and begin painting K Wing, which had not been damaged very much. After painting their fifth cell, Noel and Ian decorated a room which they thought would make a good chapel. However, in the end they were given a bigger room for a chapel, which they shared with the Education Department.

In the middle of May Noel had to go down to London in order to attend the Woolf Enquiry. Noel presented his evidence and was interviewed by Lord

Justice Woolf for about an hour and a half. The Chaplain General of Prisons was also present. After Noel had given his eye-witness evidence he was asked what his aims were in the job.

'Well,' he replied, 'we normally had five services each Sunday, for Catholics, Anglicans and Methodists.' He cleared his throat. 'Our aim was—is—rehabilitative. We want to show that men can have a different life if Christ comes into their life. They can have a life outside crime; an alternative to crime. A life of responsibility and purpose; worthwhile, with peace and happiness in it.'

Lord Justice Woolf leaned forward. 'Go on.'

'We try to make the services attractive and provoke heart-searching so that prisoners can see there's a better way.'

'What happens after the services?'

Noel said, 'After the services many men ask for counsel, or to have a talk. We can talk to them about an alternative to a life of crime, about putting their faith in Jesus Christ. Sometimes we take them to the chapel. Sometimes we see them in their cell. You see, sir, it's one of a prisoner's few rights—the right to practise his religion—and I have to co-ordinate this.' He looked straight at Lord Justice Woolf. 'You see, large numbers of men have been coming to the services. It would be sad if they have to lose this opportunity in the future because of what has happened.' He paused and dropped his gaze. He said quietly, 'But of course I'll abide by whatever is recommended.'

Lord Justice Woolf sat on for a few moments. Then he rose to show Noel and the Chaplain General, Archdeacon Keith Pound, to the door. On their way out he said to them, 'I have got no brief for this, you know.' He stopped. 'I need your prayers. Will you pray for me?'

'Oh, surely we will,' said Noel. And afterwards, as he walked away, he thought, *What a very caring man. What a humble man in such a powerful position.*

Later Noel arrived home from the station in time to go with Norma for a walk with their Yorkshire terrier, Charlie. How Noel enjoyed these walks, today especially when he told her all about Lord Justice Woolf. They both shared what had been happening in their respective days, listened to each other, unwound and generally relaxed. 'Oh, it's good to talk to you!' he cried. 'How was Heathlands?' He knew her answer before she gave it to him.

'It was lovely,' she laughed. 'I know I need to be needed, but there are so many people to help there.'

They carried on in silence and companionship. She squeezed his hand. It was good to have the old Noel back, even if it were for only a while. She remembered the letter she had written him, now in her bedside drawer, which told him about the cancer. Could she share it with him now? She glanced at him. He was happy for once, and cracking a joke about fifty per cent of his congregation turning to Christ in the first service held in the hospital waiting room. 'Fifty per cent of the congregation of prisoners. That's a better proportion than even Billy Graham gets!' he chuckled.

She entered into the spirit of things: 'And how many prisoners were in this congregation?'

'Oh, er, well, actually, two.'

'Two!' She burst out laughing.

'If one turns to the Lord that's fifty per cent, isn't it!'

She smiled and they turned towards home. She knew she could not tell him now.

'By the way,' she said, 'I've got a present for you at home.'

'Oh? And what's that?'

'You know how upset you were when the Bible I'd given you was lost and ruined in the chapel that day?'

His face went less mobile and she felt him grow tense.

'Yes?'

'Well, I've got you another one.'

'Oh Norma. That's lovely. Thank you.'

'I've written you a message inside.'

When they got home he unwrapped the Bible and read her words at the front: 'This Bible replaces the one that I gave you on our twenty-third Wedding Anniversary, and which was destroyed in the riot in Strangeways in April 1990.' She had also written:

Our God of the past. Eleven years have done great and mighty things at the prison. We rejoiced in that. Satan has tried to destroy eleven years of faithful ministry, but Jesus has promised, 'I will build my church and the gates of hell shall not prevail against it.'

Our God of the present. God has noted our tears, our questioning and our brokenness. And his love is healing us by reminding us of his promise, 'Don't struggle, but be still and know that I am God.'

Our God of the future. God assures us that after the crucifixion comes the resurrection to new life, new beginnings and new miracles. In the chaos of Strangeways stands Jesus with his arms reaching out and saying, 'Don't despair. Behold I make all things new. Heaven and earth will pass away but the word of the Lord endures for ever.' Praise God. So hang in there. Romans 8:28 is still our verse. All my love, Norma.

He turned in the new Bible to the New Testament and found Romans 8:28. 'And we know,' he read, 'that in all things God works for the good of those who love him, who have been called according to his purpose.'

What a verse, he thought. *You could spend all your life trying to plumb its depths.* He turned and looked at Norma. 'Thank you,' he said simply. 'I shall treasure this for always.' Then he went over and kissed her.

In spite of all the support received from the other chaplains who felt a deeper comradeship and brotherhood between them than ever before, and in spite of the support of the Care Team and the encouragement of the increasing number of letters and phone calls flooding in, Noel still had to cope with waves of bitterness and emptiness that could be triggered off by the tiniest thing. One day he turned from the pile of letters and frowned. Yet another person had written, kindly intentioned he knew, saying that one good result from the riot was God scattering his children from Strangeways as missionaries. Noel's brow furrowed. He felt he could not accept this. And his heart was filled with doubt.

One evening as he went into their bedroom he noticed the plaque over the bed afresh: Romans 8:28 again. 'All things working together for good . . .' *How can this be?* he said to himself, shaken by a spurt of anger. *Eleven years of blessing have collapsed at work.* Despite the 1,200 letters he was to receive all told, he simply could not see how all the horrors of the riot and siege—all the ruin of his and everyone else's work—could really and truly work together for good. How could it? He sat on the edge of the bed and slumped for a moment. Norma was out, on duty at Heathlands. He knew she believed that verse all right. She had believed it even when she had had cancer back in 1973. She had clung to it all along. She was living proof that the Bible spoke truly. He gave himself a shake, saying, 'Oh, get on with you, you idiot,' and went back to Strangeways in a slightly better frame of mind.

Another morning, as he went about his statutory duties in the prison, he was met by a lad who had been sent back to Strangeways to finish his sentence. This lad had been in the choir on the morning of 1st April and had witnessed the full force of the riot in the chapel. 'This lad is asking for you,' said a prison officer.

'Hello there,' said Noel. 'How are you? I can see they've sent you back for another dose!'

The lad flung his arms round Noel and began to cry.

'Steady there. Steady,' said Noel, gently extricating himself. 'Come on now.'

The lad managed a smile. Then he said, 'I had to tell you. You see, before the 1st of April I was not a real Christian. I know I was in the choir and that, but I was still on the touch line. But now . . . well, now I am one of the team for Jesus.'

'That's great news!' cried Noel. 'Praise the Lord!'

The lad smiled. 'I want to go straight now.'

The prison officer turned to stare at them for a moment. Then he turned back and carried on with his work.

One chaplain was to tell Noel, 'I visited a police container unit and the officer there said that he had always questioned the work of chaplains in prison until these lads had arrived from Strangeways. A number of them read their Bibles, and their behaviour was different from that of the other prisoners, and quite openly they told of how they had accepted Jesus into their lives while at Strangeways and how his power had changed them.'

So, little by little, Noel gradually came to realise that the work was still going on. This encouraged him. The encouragement slowly built up over the summer until he began to feel a lot steadier and more at peace.

One day a policeman rang the chaplaincy from Leamington Spa and said, 'I've got a lad called Will Michaels here.'

'Oh yes,' said Noel. Will, a former drug pusher and burglar, had become a Christian in prison and stuck to his faith over some months. He had led the way on the morning of the riot in rescuing the prison officer from the gang of kicking prisoners. Later he was to receive a shortening of his sentence and a Queen's Pardon. For now he had obviously been shipped out to Leamington Spa in the general dispersal of the prisoners.

The policeman said, 'I can't make him out.'

'Why's that?' asked Noel.

'Well, he's asked for a bucket of water and soap and a scrubbing brush, and he's washed his cell down and completely got rid of all the graffiti and dirt!'

Noel scratched his head, unsure of how to react.

'Then he asked for paint. So we gave him some. When I asked him what he wanted it for, he said that just because he was a prisoner it didn't mean he liked to live in filth and dirt. Anyway, I pressed him a bit more and he's told me such a tale.'

'What tale?' asked Noel.

'Oh, that Jesus has come into his life and given him a new reason for living a different life!'

'Well, that's wonderful,' said Noel, his spirits lifting.

There was a pause on the phone. 'Er, the thing is,' said the policeman, 'I never thought a prisoner, of all people, would make me think seriously about my life.'

In the moments that followed, Noel had the privilege of praying with this police officer on the phone.

When he put the phone down he was filled with joy. So some of his work had not been in vain after all.

He could not wait to get home and tell Norma about it. She was off duty when he arrived and her voice sounded tired. He grabbed Charlie's lead and called, 'Come on. Let's go for a walk.'

There was a pause and she replied, 'I'd love to, only . . .'

'Only what? Have you got a meeting?'

'No. It's not that. It's that I feel . . .' She stopped.

He waited, anxious to make the most of the evening sunshine.

'I feel rather tired today.' Her voice was low.

He looked at her in surprise. It was true; she did look tired and there was something . . . he couldn't quite make it out. Her face looked weary somehow.

'Have you got a headache?'

'Er, no darling. I'll be all right.'

Noel put the lead away. 'Come on,' he said kindly. 'You put your feet up and I'll make you a cup of tea.'

Over the tea he tried to cheer her up and by the time he'd finished, some of her old sparkle was back.

He said, 'Haven't the gang of three done us proud? Susan's passed her midwifery finals and she's working at Bradford Royal Infirmary.'

Norma nodded, remembering all her own struggles to qualify.

'And Helen's done very well in her academic work at college and has only one more teaching practice to do. And Becky. . .'

'Becky,' interrupted Norma, 'has passed all her GCSE exams with flying colours! And her first-year Sixth Form exams.'

'How come we produced such brilliance?'

They both laughed.

Twilight drew on and still they sat in a companionable silence. Noel held Norma's hand. *I hope she's all right*, he thought quietly to himself and cast a questioning look at her. He remembered how she had been at the Christmas Eve service at Elmwood Church the previous December, as if she were labouring under some strong emotion. He had assumed that she was all right. But now he was not sure. He had been so involved with the riot and its aftermath that, as he suddenly realised, he had not really had the time or the opportunity to think about how Norma might be feeling. His hand tightened around hers. *From now on,* he thought, *I'm going to make sure she's all right.*

13

Living with Cancer

The weeks went by. Soon it was high summer and then early autumn was looming. Noel continued to work daily in the prison. He found that in common with other chaplaincy team members, officers and inmates it was hard to come to any definite conclusions about anything as far as their emotions were concerned. Inmates were really suffering from overcrowding in the police cells in and around Manchester; parents and families of other prisoners sent away as far as the South of England had all the problems of travelling to visit them. Many people suffered for months with emotional and psychological hurt as a result of the trauma of the riot. Some staff were sent on detached duty around the area. Some were transferred to other jobs; their children had to be uprooted from school and their houses put up for sale. This affected families deeply. The chaplaincy did all it could to support others. Ian Ferguson was moved to Stafford Prison. Everyone missed him, especially Noel, as they had worked together for so many years.

By early autumn there were just under fifty inmates, housed in the hospital and employed as cleaners and workers in the kitchen and the mess. These prisoners were allowed some free association and videos, so it gave Noel a lot of encouragement that a fair number chose to come to the Bible classes, discussion groups or fellowship groups. Once over half the inmates came to a meeting; two lads made a commitment to Christ. Then K Wing was almost ready to take about 150 inmates and Noel knew that this would ease the pressure in police cells around Manchester. He had a chapel made out of six cells knocked into one; people sent gifts of hymn books, other books and money. He knew that there was still a work to be done in Strangeways. In the middle of all this, after the Woolf Enquiry was over, they were told that Manchester Prison was coming up for 'market testing'. Everything was up in the air, pointing towards a new era. No one knew if he or she would still have a job in the months or years to come. It did not help to ease the pressure, tension and heartache of life inside.

At home Noel was quieter than usual. He and Norma carried on with all their normal activities. Norma greatly enjoyed her local church, St Paul's. She had a good group of friends there, who had all prayed and worked together, especially after the church was burned down a few years before. They met in the school while the church was being rebuilt. The new vicar, Stephen Fletcher, began house groups and slowly the church grew. One evening, at the Wednesday prayer meeting, Norma had a vision. She tried to explain it to the others there. 'There's a boat. A big stately galleon with bright colours and it's very strong. There are people hanging out of all the windows, and over the decks, with hands out-stretched. Oh!' She paused. 'And the water is full of other people, desperate to be rescued, some swimming and some sinking. The people on the boat are pulling them in, rescuing them. Oh! It's wonderful. Everything is so brilliantly coloured.' There was a long silence. Finally she said, 'I believe that the boat is us, at St Paul's. We mustn't give up, whatever we do, because we have such a ministry of helping and rescuing people.'

Noel was still up when she came back at one o'clock in the morning, her face completely lit up. He listened and rejoiced with her. *I haven't got what she has got in the way of spiritual gifts*, he thought. But his heart lifted and he was thrilled on her behalf. Then he watched as she set off upstairs to go to bed. She stopped halfway up, pausing for breath. She coughed again. He knew she had been coughing a lot lately. He ran up the stairs and gave her his arm. Later, when she was asleep, he still lay awake. She looked so tired lately. He turned over. Perhaps their planned weekend away at Barnard Castle, visiting old friends from their County Durham days, would help. Yet in his heart, deep down, without him naming it to himself, Noel was beginning to realise what was wrong with Norma. He knew too that he would wait until she was ready to tell him about it.

In retrospect, this weekend was a turning point in their lives. There was no going back as far as the cancer was concerned and in the end Noel did ask her what was the matter, as she spent so much time coughing and having trouble catching her breath as she went upstairs.

Afterwards Norma wrote about their experience in her journal:

Now it's September. Please God, let me live until December for Helen's graduation. I am living for Helen's graduation, and with that over, I would be at peace. Oh, I would love to be around for Becky's graduation, for their weddings, for my grandchildren, but I don't ask for that.

I have had a dry irritating cough for some weeks now and I am breathless when I climb stairs or go up an incline. I know my condition is worsening, but I want to keep it hidden from my family for just a while longer. When Helen finishes her teaching practice, then I will tell them how ill I am.

Noel and I have had a few days' holiday in Co. Durham, visiting old haunts and old friends from parish days. My cough has been particularly troublesome and I know I haven't looked well. Noel, I so want to tell you I am ill, but you have been through so much, how can I heap more sorrow on you?

Then one evening Noel said, 'Norma, is this cough worrying you?' and I told him as gently as I could of the secondary spread. I am amazed, as he looked at me and said, 'Yes, I know. I just wondered when you would tell me.' I explained to Noel that the only treatment on offer to me was chemotherapy, and I know about cytotoxic (anti-cancer) drugs and their awful side-effects. I have always said that I want quality in my life, not quantity.[1]

We loved and cuddled each other and we wept together and committed it to the Lord. Noel knows I'm no quitter. I shall fight in God's strength for a while longer. When the time is right, we shall tell the girls.

No bitterness, no struggling, no more rebellion. At times I feel weary, at times exhilarated, but always grateful to God for today—tomorrow I must trust him for.

How I thank God for my work at Heathlands, for my colleagues, for the fellowship we enjoy together. Heathlands helps me to forget about myself, as there are so many patients and staff who need me. Inherent in me is the need to be needed; to reach out and touch somebody else.

I try not to think that I'm dying with cancer, rather that I'm living with cancer. God's grace is available to me each day and I'm taking it one day at a time.

It's wonderful to have Noel's loving support and to be able to be open with him. Please God, I ask again that you will spare me to see Helen's graduation!

As I look back on my life, I have had so much: loving parents, grandparents, family relatives, a good marriage, a loving and devoted husband, three beautiful and talented daughters. I have been totally fulfilled.

On the way home from Barnard Castle they called in to see Susan in Leeds. As soon as Susan saw her mother looking so shocking, she became suspicious about her mother's health. She managed to take Noel on one side and asked him outright what was the matter. He sat down suddenly at the table and tears flowed down his cheeks. Susan guessed straightaway that Norma must have a secondary spread of cancer. 'And the only thing that's keeping her going is Helen's graduation,' said Noel. He shook his head. 'Why didn't she tell us?'

Susan put her arms around him. 'Because she wanted to spare us,' she said, wiping the tears away from her own eyes. 'I'd better pretend I don't know yet,' she said after a while. 'Perhaps next time I'm home for the weekend, she'll tell me then.' She looked at her father. 'Look, Dad, I think you'll have to carry on at work. She won't want you brooding at home, will she?'

He looked at his hands. 'No, she won't. No, I'll carry on as long as possible.'

On 30th September Noel drove to the Lake District to spend the night at Newby Bridge. The next day he was to watch Barry Cuttle (a Manchester solicitor) and his son and daughter do a sponsored relay swim from Newby Bridge to Appleton on Lake Windermere, which was to raise £10,000 for the work of the chaplaincy. Noel smiled momentarily to himself as he drove up the motorway with the POA Chairman and Secretary, remembering clearly one night near the beginning of the siege of Strangeways. He had been negotiating with prisoners to get them to come down off the roof and surrender. Barry Cuttle had been in the team of negotiators. In a lull Barry had suddenly said quietly to Noel: 'What's happened to your organ in the chapel?'

Noel replied, 'Well, if the prisoners didn't destroy it, the Fire Brigade certainly have because they've poured so much water in!'

Barry looked him straight in the eye. 'I'll get you a new one,' he said.

Noel laughed. He knew people *thought* they meant what they said at 2 o'clock in the morning, but he always took such things with a pinch of salt. Tomorrow would be another day.

Barry said, 'No, I mean it. I'll do a sponsored swim for you.'

Barry had been as good as his word, and now Noel was on his way to watch him.

Noel booked into the hotel for all three of them. He and Ivor Serle had to share a room and by 10.00pm Ivor had settled down and was ready for a good night's rest. But something was strange in the room. Ivor lay still and tried to work out what it was. All at once he realised it was the quietness that was so intense. In fact it was so quiet that he could not get to sleep. Ivor turned over and saw Noel kneeling by his bed, praying he guessed. Noel was so quiet; he never made a sound. Ivor turned back again, but sleep eluded him.

In the end he took another look at Noel, who had now got into bed and was reading his Bible. By this time the sense of quiet was unbelievable, and with it came something else. There was a peace too in the room. And in that hotel room near Lake Windermere something said to him, 'Ivor, you've got to have some of that peace. You talk to Noel about it in the morning.'

Later Noel was to write about this time in Ivor's life:

That morning, as we were making our way down to the place where the swim was to take off, Ivor said to me, 'I'd like to be baptised, Noel.' And I looked at him and I said, 'Ivor, for an adult to be baptised you've got to commit your life to Jesus. Are you ready to do that?' And he said to me, 'I think so.'

Nothing more was said. I had no chapel. We were having our services in the Officers' Club, surrounded by bottles of whisky and beer, so it was 'real thirst after righteousness'! But a few days later Ivor said to me, 'Have you done anything about arranging my baptism?'

I said, 'No, I want to talk to you first,' and so we went down to the Christian World Centre and had our dinner one day.

I said to him, 'Why do you want to be baptised?' At that time Norma was very ill, and Ivor said to me, 'I have watched you through the riot and before the riot. I've watched you as you've looked after the staff and the prisoners through these difficult times. I've seen you with your dungarees on painting cells and doing jobs that I never expected from you.' And he added, 'Now you've got a wife who's ill. If your faith can give you that courage and that strength to cope the way you have done, I want that faith.'

I felt really humbled by what Ivor said. We went into the little studio at Christian World and I explained to him step by step what it meant to commit your life to Jesus, and that day Ivor knelt with me in the little studio and he asked the Lord Jesus to come into his life.

A few weeks later we borrowed a church at Blackley and his friends came and we had the baptism, and Ivor shared with the people before he was baptised why he was being baptised. Yes, perhaps if the riot meant nothing else but that Ivor Serle should come to a place in his life where he wanted to put Jesus first, well that was worthwhile.

Meanwhile life had to carry on at home. Norma continued to write her journal, glad that she had been able to be open with Noel at last. There was a peace, she found, in knowing that he knew and that he loved her. She felt a sense of calling in the writing and did not really know how to explain it. But she knew that she almost had a duty and a purpose in the writing. She guessed that somehow some of it might get into print one day, and that as she had something to say, she really had to take out the old-fashioned yellow-cornered and hard-backed journal and put herself into it. So she sat up in bed many evenings during the autumn and wrote it all down:

So much has happened in the last few weeks. Susan came home for the weekend and it was wonderful to see her, but she notices the change. Becky has told her, 'Mum is always tired these days.' So Sue asked Noel and he told her—she is devastated. At bedtime Noel told me that Susan knows and so I went into her room and embraced my first born and we sobbed together.

'Mum, I don't understand God's dealings with you and Dad. Strangeways' riot has crushed you both, but why this? Dad will be torn apart.' I expect all our lives we will keep asking why, especially in the dark areas of our experiences ... so many questions unanswered. What is faith if it is not reaching out into the darkness of doubt and despair, crying,

'Lord, I don't understand, but hold on to me for I trust you, Lord'?

Sue wrote to Alan and Flo, two more people who have befriended us all these past eleven years. They surrounded us with their prayers.

Stephen Fletcher, our Rector, called and we shared with him what we were going through. Stephen was so sensitive and caring.

I asked for a healing service in our home on the Wednesday and asked to be anointed with oil, according to the Scriptures. Noel asked that he be anointed with oil also. Wednesday came and my closest friends Annie, Alan and Flo, Stephen, Noel and I met in our lounge. God's peace was already filling my heart and mind. We had a time of praise and worship, then three readings from Scripture; a time of confession and waiting upon God followed, then they each in turn anointed Noel and me with oil, and the sign of the cross was made on our foreheads.

Stephen asked me to sit for this, but I felt compelled to kneel, for after all I was in the very presence of the King of kings.

It was a wonderful time and I felt so blessed. I was surrounded by those who loved me and longed for my healing.

Jesus, we all must face our Gethsemane in life and even in the midst of the sadness, like you I caught a glimpse of your glory. Praise God!

Note

[1] Since Norma was first diagnosed in 1973 the treatments and options available to cancer patients have come on in leaps and bounds. The options and side-effects of cytotoxic (anti-cancer) treatment in the 1990s offer much more hope

and promise than they ever did. The choice of the management of cancer is an individual choice; many complexities have to be taken into account, based on a spectrum of factors. Not to have chemotherapy the second time round was Norma's individual choice. Her objection was not to drugs or medical treatment as such (which can include surgery, antibiotics, iron), but to the anti-cancer drugs and their side-effects. Keeping her dignity right to the very end was very important to her. She did not have anti-cancer drugs, but she did receive some other types of drug treatment towards the end.

Susan Proctor MSc, RGN, RM

14

Norma's Journal

How I thank God for my friends. How kind and caring they are—and how discreet. Today Annie called with some home baking; such practical Christianity.

Yesterday I felt really off colour. So tired and weary. 'Oh God, give me some energy. I want to live fully whatever time is left. Thank you, Jesus.'

Noel, bless him, so warm and loving, keeps his thoughts and feelings hidden. He is so grateful to God for each day we have. 'Lord, in my anxiety, I plead that you will spare my life for a little longer. Please don't crush Noel.' Then I realise I see things with only limited sight. I see only my situation. I need to pray for wider vision, knowing that God sees the whole panorama of our lives. He is the Alpha and the Omega. 'Lord, I surrender to you. You are in control of my situation. Thank you, Lord.'

Helen phoned. Her teaching practice is going well. She is happy. Thank God.

Becky is busy sorting out her choice of university. God, guide them all. I remember my grandmother's philosophy from many years ago: 'Those whom God guides are well guided.'

Today I told Bridget Salmon, my colleague for eleven years. She and I are like chalk and cheese, but we have a good relationship. Today we wept together, we embraced and held onto each other. Bridget reminded me: 'Norma, God is love and he loves you. Fight on in his name.' How I thank God for my friend. Over our working years we have laughed together and remained loyal to each other in the nursing profession. Bridget tried to impart some of her strength to me, but most of all she promised to pray for me.

Today I feel so weary. I look around the home that I love and I want to do so much, but my energy is spent. I had a phone call from a Jewish friend to tell me her husband is suffering from lung cancer and is now very poorly indeed and is on a morphine drip. Poor man, not long retired and now this. Is it wrong to ask what life is all about?

Someone has said: 'Faith is trusting when we can't understand,' but at times it's almost impossible. 'Oh God, help me to hold onto you!'

My heart aches for Noel. He tries to be cheerful, going about his duties. Yesterday, he took the funeral of a fifty-three-year-old prison officer who died very suddenly from a massive heart attack. He visited the family, trying to impart some comfort to them—it can't have been easy.

Noel, you know how much I love you and how precious these twenty-six years have been. I have a husband who is very special and I treasure him. 'A marriage made in heaven.' Thank God that over our relationship is the stamp of his approval.

It's good to reach out in the night and hear words of comfort and reassurance; to feel Noel take hold of my hand and squeeze it, just to let me know he cares.

'Lord, minister to Noel. Impart your strength and grace to him. He gives himself unsparingly to all.

Anoint us both in your Holy Spirit. Jesus, I'm tired, but I rest in you. Thank you for your peace.'

I told Bill Sheehan, the nursing officer at Heathlands, how ill I am. He was shocked, but practical and supportive. Susan is home for the weekend and, bless her, she takes over in the kitchen. She has told Becky about me. She says that she modified it for her. So now only Helen needs to be told, and if God spares me I will wait until the end of her teaching practice.

I went with Susan and Becky to a craft fair at the school today. Normally I would stay for ages looking at the stalls, but I felt too weary to look around.

So many people are praying for me. How I thank God for the power of prayer.

I am going by coach to Margie my sister in Hampshire for a few days. I'm not looking forward to the long coach journey, but I know it will be worth it just to be together and put the world to rights. Margie phoned to say that a girl who works with her, after being told about me, had given her a vial of Holy Water from Lourdes for my use. However different our theology might be I was really touched by the kindness of this woman reaching out to me in love. God can only be exalted by such action.

Susan is on leave and will be home for a few days to look after Noel and Becky.

The few days I spent with Margie were wonderful. I was treated like royalty. Everyone was so kind and attentive. It was good just to be with my sister, who, bless her, put on a brave face and tried so hard to be positive. I never realised how much she loved me, and I hid my tears from her. She said, 'Noel and you are such a special team. No one thinks of one without the other. So I cannot believe that God will split the two of you. You have so much more to do for him.'

She was so sincere in what she said that I wanted so much to believe it—but life isn't that simple. We parted at the coach station and her reserve crumbled and she wept openly. I hated being the cause of her grief.

Noel told me he had had a visit from Bridget, my colleague, who wanted to talk to him about me, and they'd finished off praying together. Such warmth and depth of feeling. People are so kind.

Helen is home from teaching practice for just a few days. I must try to be strong and keep up the pretence of all being well. I will tell her when the time is right.

I feel so weak. I wish my appetite would improve. It seems strange to me, for however poorly I have been in the past I could always eat. I don't want to burden my family and friends. I long for healing; to be stronger. And even if I don't ask 'why?' with my lips, my heart is continually questioning.

'O Lord, I don't pretend to understand and I hate how I feel, so in this darkness, Lord, I reach out my hand to you. Just hold me tight. I love you, Jesus, but I don't understand your dealings with me.'

Tonight our friends are meeting in our home to pray with Noel and me, and to minister to us. The rector has brought bread and wine so we can celebrate the Holy Communion service.

It was a wonderful evening. Noel and I shared how we felt. My own feelings were quite mixed. A few days previously we had been to town, my first visit for weeks, and in walking along Market Street we had to stop three times so I might rest. It was discouraging for me and I felt so low. As usual I voiced what I felt before my God (I never see the need for pretence before him, for his word tells me that he knows what I'm thinking) and in my frustration I cried, 'Lord, if this is living, please let me die. I don't want to feel perpetually weary. I want to live.' On the Wednesday of the meeting I felt really good. Emotional, but at peace. Before we parted, we sang 'In the name of Jesus, we have the victory'!

Next day I felt poorly and vomited twice, in spite of having eaten next to nothing. Noel read to me Psalm 103 from the Living Bible and I was comforted.

Helen has an interview at a school in Barnsley on Monday 5th November. The references from her present teaching practice are glowing. God *is* in control of our lives.

I thank God for Noel—so patient and caring, and for darling Becky who is at home and sees me at my worst. How I wish I could spare them.

Noel visited the Isle of Man yesterday to speak at two meetings on the invitation of the Chief Constable, Robin Oakes. He enjoyed his time there and spoke of the friendliness and warmth of the people. At last evening's meeting, an elderly gentleman asked him where I was, said he had read *The Cross Behind Bars* three times and that I had inspired him. I felt quite humbled that I should inspire anyone, but God uses us all and I felt encouraged that somehow I had been of help to this man. Noel said I had been prayed for most earnestly. I knew it, for I slept so well and felt so at peace.

When Noel returned home at about 8.00am this morning, the first thing he did was to offer thanks to God that we were together again. No wonder I love him so much!

This morning I am off duty and from my bedroom I hear the happy noise of children on their way to school. I have been talking with the Lord and listening to him. I was reading Psalm 34 in the night.

Verses 8–9 are beautiful with the promises of God. I have asked him to touch my cancerous body. I so long to be healed; to waken to vitality.

What is it about us that when people ask us how we feel we say 'fine'? This morning my defences were down and when Noel asked, I wanted to drop the façade and say, 'I feel rotten, weary and despondent,' but why add to his burdens?

I don't need a façade with the Lord. He sees right into my heart. He doesn't see me as a wife and mother, or as a ward sister. He sees me as his weak and vulnerable child, and he cuddles me in his love. 'Lord, I need your strength. Just hold me and let me know you are with me always.'

My dear colleague Bridget and my wonderful friend Judy convince me to see a specialist. I saw a very human and compassionate man, who, when he examined me, confirmed all I already knew. He referred me to Christie Hospital. My first visit is to be in early December.

Norma left her job at Heathlands by the end of November. Her cough was worse, and fluid in her stomach made her feel uncomfortable, even causing her to vomit at times. Finally she plucked up the courage to speak to Helen:

I told Helen as gently as I could and tried not to alarm her. She was naturally anxious.

I was apprehensive about going to Christie's and yet I need not have been. Dr Stewart, the consultant, was positive and so easy to talk to. I discovered later that he was a committed Christian. He had several X-rays taken and said that there was fluid on my left lung that would need draining, after which he would start hormone treatment.

So I was admitted for a few days for scanning, X-rays and chest aspiration. The drug I was prescribed was new, and I was to be a 'guinea pig'. *Please God*, I thought, *let it work for me*. It didn't—I was so sick constantly that I was becoming dehydrated. My appetite was non-existent, for whatever I ate just wouldn't stay down. The drug was changed and thankfully I began to eat a little.

Becky and Susan went on several long walks and finally Susan said as gently as she could, 'Mum won't be around for my birthday next June. That's what we've got to face. Together.'

'I've known really,' said Becky and thrust her hands into her pockets. 'And I know how serious it is.'

'Yes.' Susan thought about her mother and how uncomfortable she must be: the cough affected her at night and the nausea all day. The fluid affected her stomach and the rest of her was wasting away. 'Come on, Becky. Let's go home.'

December came, and with it all the Christmas preparations. First, however, there was Helen's graduation at Leeds University. Norma had been literally living for this day and took trouble with her hair, her make-up and her clothes. Noel became anxious when Helen explained to him about the vast flight of stairs up to the main hall where the ceremony was to take place. When they arrived and looked up the stairs, Noel knew that Norma would never make it. He rushed round to see if there was a lift, but could find nothing. 'I *will* get up there,' said Norma with the old, determined glint in her eye.

Eventually, while Helen went off to robe, a couple of strangers came along and between them half-carried and half-supported Norma in a fireman's lift until she was in the Great Hall, and seated more or less comfortably.

Helen graduated on 18th December at Leeds University. I felt so ill that day, but nothing was stopping me from going to the proud event. Helen looked lovely. So young, so full of life. I was a proud mother and so thankful to God that I had been spared to see this day.

Christmas was almost upon us. Susan took over the Christmas shopping. Helen cleaned and decorated the house and everywhere looked lovely.

Susan was working until 2.00pm on Christmas Day, so Helen and Becky cooked the dinner. It was lovely to be together as a family.

In January I began to feel poorly again and noticed my abdomen was swollen. I was taken into Christie's again and 1.5 gallons of fluid were aspirated from my tummy. I felt so weak. I couldn't stand and became very despondent. I was inundated with cards and flowers and the assurance of hundreds praying for me. Yet in the darkness I cried out, 'Lord, have you forgotten me?' Immediately his words came: 'A mother may forget the child she bears, but I will never forget you. I have carved you on the palms of my hands.'

Susan and Noel knew how much it meant to Norma to keep her dignity, particularly while she was in hospital. Everyone in the family respected her decision as far as the chemotherapy was concerned. It was hard for Norma to accept that part of the treatment for removing the fluid from her stomach was to take water tablets, which meant she had to keep asking for bed pans or the commode. It mortified her to sit on the commode with only screens around her bed.

Once Norma came home again she was very weak. She had to be turned constantly, and although she never complained of pain she was in a lot of discomfort.

Often Becky came home early from college, anxious to help. She knew she would not be able to move Norma on her own, so she would ring their friend Flo Eccles, from the corner, who would come round and help. The most difficult thing Becky found was that her mother kept apologising to her for interrupting her 'A' level studies. *I don't mind. I want to help you*, thought Becky. *My 'A' levels will be all right. Please don't keep saying you are sorry*. But poor Norma did not realise and Becky did not know how to tell her.

Noel too got himself into the new routine. He knew that Norma wanted him to keep on working and not to brood, so he arrived at Strangeways for 7.30am. By 9 o'clock he was back home, giving Norma her breakfast and settling her down for the morning. He drove back to work, and then returned for lunch so that they could eat it together. It was a punishing schedule and one day he nearly fainted at work. However, he decided to keep going. What else was he to do?

Many afternoons Flo or Annie, Norma's two close friends nicknamed 'the golden girls', came round to see her. She had the phone by her bed if she needed help and Becky was always home late afternoon, if not before.

The staff of Heathlands were also a great support, not only to Norma, but to the whole family. They often brought gifts of food and flowers. A wheelchair and oxygen, bedding and food supplements were all provided by the nursing home.

Norma herself always made an effort to see visitors when they called. Her faith was unshakeable, although she always kept her feet firmly planted on the ground. Susan says, 'She still had her doubts and fears, the anguishes and the physical horrors that go along with cancer, but that love she had for the Lord just sustained her. Her faith was incredibly strong. She felt she had been given eighteen Christian years that she did not deserve. Each of those years was a gift and a blessing in her eyes.'

Noel says, 'She often spoke about the eighteen years we had had together to see the girls grow up. This was what we had asked for initially. Those eighteen years were very precious to her.'

Noel was ashamed of his own reactions to Norma's cancer back in 1973 when he had not really felt able to confide in anyone. This time he did not make the same mistake. Staff and prisoners knew, and he found that this helped. There was always someone to call on if he felt he could not cope: friends, hospital, prison staff, church, Heathlands, the girls. They were all there when he needed them.

Norma continued to write, although often she felt too weak to put down much. It became a struggle for her to write in this journal, so she did it in fits and starts, always determined to finish:

Discharged from Christie's again, thankfully eating and it's staying down—moving around slowly but surely, and ready for my next check-up in two weeks' time.

People have been so kind, offering help in so many ways. The feeling of being dependent, however, is awful. I have good days and bad days. Someone was discussing with me from Romans 12, knowing what is 'that good acceptable and perfect will of God'. I confessed that God's will had not been acceptable to me. I questioned his dealings, then I was reminded again of Jesus on the night before his crucifixion saying, 'Father, if it be possible, let this cup pass from me. Nevertheless, not my will but yours be done.' If Jesus found the acceptability of his Father's will difficult, then who was Norma Proctor to find it otherwise?

Helen has got her teaching post in Barnsley. Susan has a new boyfriend. Becky hopes to go to Edinburgh University if her 'A' level results are favourable.

I take one day at a time. There is some improvement, but I'm holding onto Jesus with all I have.

Noel struggled on through that winter of 1991. Even when spring began to show signs of new growth he felt as if he were in the dark; in a prison in his own mind. One day he said:

I remember when Norma was very ill in February 1991. It was a Sunday morning and Becky rang just after the services were over to say that Norma couldn't get her breath—could I get home? I rushed home, and sure enough the fluid was gathering in her lungs and she couldn't breathe. I rang up Christie Hospital and they said they would send an ambulance out. Within three-quarters of an hour the ambulance was there. The ambulancemen came in and they wrapped her in a blanket. They put her in the carrying-chair, and then perhaps this was the point that really hurt most of all. They put the blanket round her head to carry her out to the ambulance because of the snow and the sleet.

Norma had always said that she wanted dignity when she died—one of the reasons why she wouldn't have chemotherapy. That day, as they carried her out, something seemed to go inside me. Suddenly I was really angry. Angry with a God who I knew loved me and cared for me. I knew he had brought me through all these experiences down the years, but I was angry because Norma seemed to be losing her dignity, when the one thing she wanted was that. As I followed the ambulance in the car to Christie Hospital the Lord and myself had a real row. I couldn't help but argue with him. 'What are you doing? What are you playing at? She wants a little bit of dignity in her death, in her last days. Why can't you give it to her? What kind of God are you?' And so I went on. Perhaps I needed some of my anti-swearing tablets, because there were some terrible words coming out as the tears were running down my face in the car that day. The hurt that was inside me was bubbling out and I couldn't take it out on anyone else except the God I worshipped.

We got Norma settled into the ward and I never said anything to her about what was happening. She knew deep down that I was hurting very much. I left her that night and when I came home Becky was there in the house, but I was tired. I went to bed, but I couldn't sleep. I couldn't say my prayers. I knew that between me and God there was a barrier. Something was wrong in our relationship, and I knew that I was the one who had caused it. He wasn't a God of hardness, he wasn't a God of cruelty, he wasn't a God of discipline. He was a God who was trying to teach me, and I found it hard to learn.

That night, as I lay in my bed, there was no sleep. I tossed and I turned. Oh, I was hurting so much. In the early hours of the morning I was very conscious of a presence in the bedroom. Becky was in her own bedroom, but in our bedroom there was a presence. Not a presence of awe and holiness, not a presence of hardness or discipline or pressure, but a presence of care, a presence of love, a presence that was reaching out to me, a presence that was so close I could feel it. And as clear as crystal I heard a voice saying, 'Stop your fighting, stop your struggling. She's mine and I love her. Give her to me. I'll look after her.'

When I got up in the morning I was at peace. I couldn't explain why. I'd had no rest, yet I was at peace. I got myself sorted out and went off to

Christie Hospital to see Norma. By then they had taken fluid off her lungs and she was feeling better. I told her what had happened. I told her of the fight and the argument and the row that I had had with the Lord. Perhaps I was a bit like Job of old. I had to come to dust and ashes before I realised his presence and his power.

And when I'd told her the story she started to laugh at me. She said, 'I knew you were fighting with the Lord, but there's no point. Jesus has given us these eighteen years to see our girls grow up; to see our girls give their lives to Jesus; to give us great blessing in our ministry. We have seen so many wonderful things happening and we have known his presence and his blessing. Now we have always known that he could call us home. We have always known that this sword of Damocles has been hanging over us. I am ready to go. And God has got a new ministry for you,' she said. 'Why don't you let him give it to you?' I have thought of these words often.

Yet it was strange in the weeks that followed. I clutched at every straw. One night I returned from the convent after being at a prayer meeting. Susan, Helen and Becky were with their mum, and little Sister Anne had talked about a man over in Dublin who was a healer, who could even pray with people on the telephone and these people had been healed. And that night when I came home we got on the telephone to Dublin. He wasn't in. He had gone out to a prayer meeting, but he would be in at 9 o'clock the following morning. The amazing thing was that where Norma was concerned she was content. As she said, she had no pain—she had discomfort, but no pain—and she was ready to go to the Lord. But I was fighting, I was struggling.

The following morning, just after 9 o'clock, we rang Dublin again and this brother came on the phone and he talked to Norma and he talked to me. And he prayed with us both. I suppose I was expecting too much. Norma wasn't. She knew. She had accepted the fact that she was going to be with the Lord Jesus and she was ready to go. And in many ways she wanted to go. She prepared her own funeral service and the rector of our parish came regularly to bring us communion. She even prepared the talk that he gave and the hymns that were sung. It was all as if she knew it was coming and it was all going down in this book that she was writing since the day of the riot—her memoirs, or her journal as she called it, which she continued to write until three weeks before she died.

15
Norma Goes Home

Nothing can ever separate us from his love.
Death can't, and life can't . . . (Rom
8:37—Living Bible).

For their twenty-seventh Wedding Anniversary in
March Susan bought her parents a baby alarm. This
was set up near Norma, who was sleeping downstairs
by now so that she could indicate if she needed help.
Noel found he could hardly sleep because he could hear
her as she coughed throughout most nights and her
breathing was loud and laboured.

She struggled over her last few journal entries:

Time has passed and now it is April. Many visits to
Christie Hospital to have fluid drained from my
lungs and abdomen. Dr Stewart is always helpful
and honest—he pulls no punches and raises no false
hopes.

The initial weeks were dreadful, the treatment
made me so ill. I lost three stone and looked awful.

Today the 20th April. I have good days and bad
ones. I know hundreds are still praying for my
healing and I am comforted.

As a family we have talked quite openly about
death, for healing is not only physical but spiritual.
When I came home from my last stay at Christie's,

157

the dining room had been made into a bedroom for me. No more climbing stairs. It's a haven and I feel God's presence with me at all times.

Noel said he has stopped struggling with the Lord over my healing. He had wept so often seeing my weakness and then one night he told the Lord, 'I hand Norma over to you, Lord. No more pleading and struggling. You are in control of our situation and I leave her with you.' He told me of an indescribable peace filling his heart and the very presence of God filling his room.

I awakened the other night to hear the words of St Paul echoing in my bedroom. 'I have fought a good fight. I have finished the course. I have kept the faith, henceforth there is laid up for me a crown of righteousness which the Lord, the righteous judge, will give me and not to me only, but to all who love his appearing.'

I know I am dying, as my family know it too, but I am in his hands. I am not struggling, only resting in him.

Does this mean I understand his dealings with me? No! Does it mean I no longer want to live? No! But I trust my God. Many of my questions are not going to be answered this side of eternity. We see only through a darkened glass, but one day we shall see Jesus and the darkness will pass away.

'The Son of God who loved me and gave himself for me' (Galations 2:20).

I have lived a fulfilled life—as a woman, a nurse, a wife, a mother, and above all as a follower of Jesus Christ since I was thirteen years old.

No one has been more loved. No one has been made to feel so complete.

Noel Proctor is the only man I have ever loved and I could not begin to describe his devotion to me.

Noel is and has been God's precious gift to me. Our relationship has the stamp of God's approval all over it.

This is what I pray my girls will find—fulfilment in life and completeness in their Saviour.

Norma's journal was to end here.

On the early May Spring Bank Holiday Monday Norma was able to go to the opening of the 'new' St Paul's Church, Kersal Moor, finally rebuilt after fire had destroyed it four years previously. With Noel's help and the aid of a wheelchair she gazed up at the building and her face filled with delight and memories. She recalled how long they had been going to this their parish church; how the congregation had had to meet in the school after the fire; how a new young vicar and his wife and children had come and had guided the church into meeting in house groups; how a new unity had sprung up between them all and the church had really grown.

Inside, the church was resplendent with its new interior, the flowers and the happiness of the people who had worked, given and prayed for its arising from the ashes of the fire and despair. 'Take me to see the new window of the Holy Spirit,' Norma asked, and Noel pushed her over. She sat and gazed at it for some time.

Afterwards, as they were leaving, she said, 'I want my ashes buried just outside the church door.' Noel nodded and squeezed her hand.

By this time Norma was too weak to continue writing, so Noel and Susan contrived writing on her behalf:

Norma is now too weak to walk the short distance from her bed in the dining room to the settee in the lounge, so Heathlands have loaned us a wheelchair, which means to get her moved she puts her arms around my neck and waist and I lift her onto the chair. As long as her knees don't buckle, we can manage, but her legs are swollen up with fluid and are very heavy.

Bridget, her colleague from Heathlands, has had to go to Trinidad as her mother is seriously ill. Norma is missing her visits, but Bridget has rung a couple of times and these calls have given Norma real encouragement.

We had a long talk one evening after our prayers about the subject of death. Norma has no fear of it, only of the process of dying, and all its indignities. She was anxious to talk to the girls about it, especially Helen and Becky. She spoke to Helen on the Saturday and it resulted in them both experiencing a closer bond of union than they already had.

Becky and I talked about death and how that as Mum is drawing near to it we must keep our eyes on Jesus. I knew Becky's mind was full of questions . . . mine was as well.

It was Saturday evening and Norma was in bed in the dining room, surrounded by her family photos and her antiques gathered over the years. We had our own prayer time together and suddenly she said, 'I haven't heard you singing round the house lately.' My reply was that there hadn't been much to sing about. She said, 'Sing "Great is thy faithfulness".' I did try, but after a couple of lines I broke down in tears. Suddenly her weak voice took over and encouraged me to sing on. Helen came in and played the piano. It was nearly 11.30pm when we finished praising and worshipping the Lord Jesus. As I climbed the stairs I could not help but admire her strength and faith.

Norma was never in any pain, for which we thank God, but she had a lot of discomfort from the fluid gathering in her tummy, legs and lungs. Her continual coughing was sapping what little strength she had left. On Sunday 19th May I was supposed to preach at Lymm, but rang to make my excuses and stayed with Norma.

Susan was with me to help care for Norma and on Monday, as her cough had become so distressing, Sue called for Dr Smith, the GP, to visit. Sue mentioned to Norma and me that he may suggest she be admitted for professional care, in a hospice. When he came he did discuss this option with us and appropriate arrangements were made. We had a phone call from St Ann's Hospice in Heald Green to say they would have a bed on Tuesday morning.

Monday night was difficult. Sue and I were up with Norma for most of the night. She was distressed because of her cough, uncomfortable because of the fluid and so very, very tired and weak. At one point when we came to her she was saying, 'I want my mummy.' I got really worried, but Sue reassured me that this often happens when people are seriously ill.

Perhaps the humour of the situation came through when at 7.45am Norma called for me. She wanted to know why I was not getting her ready for the ambulancemen who were due at 10.00am. I found Sue asleep in the lounge—she hadn't even managed to get back up the stairs to her own bed after being up with Norma all night! Together we bed-bathed Norma and got her ready for her journey.

Sue went with her in the ambulance and I followed on later. At St Ann's Hospice the love and genuine concern were beautiful and Norma was clearly at ease and had peace of mind.

I collected Becky from college at 3.00pm and we went out to see Norma. She was very weary and drowsy and after a time asked us to leave. She made us promise to ring her when we got news of Helen's interview for a new teaching post in Sowerby Bridge near Halifax. This must have been playing on Norma's mind, for she asked Pat McEvoy (a friend) to ring later that evening for some news.

Helen rang at 9.00pm to say that she had got the job and I at once rang the hospice. The chap on the switchboard said he would go and tell Norma.

At 10.30pm the night sister rang to say that Norma's breathing was difficult, but an injection had been given and she was settling down. I asked to be kept informed and I would come if she felt it necessary.

At 11.10pm the phone rang again and I was asked to come. I reassured Becky and told her to go to bed and that I would be back soon.

When I arrived there, Norma had already passed away in her sleep. I sat at the bedside and read aloud to her, her favourite passage, Romans 8, sobbing as I moved from promise to promise in those wonderful verses. I looked at Norma and perhaps it was the light or the fact that I had just kissed her on the lips, but she appeared to be smiling—she was in the presence of the Lord Jesus whom she loved so much.

Norma was the first person to be buried at the 'new' St Paul's. Her funeral took place on Wednesday 29th May 1991. Stephen Fletcher took it, working from Norma's own plans, which Noel had written down. The church was packed; there was standing room only at the back. The road outside was clogged with the parked cars and coaches of the mourners. Yet Norma would not have wanted anyone to grieve when she herself had passed into the presence of her Lord and Saviour. Although there was deep sadness and sorrow during the service, by the end came a surge of uplifting as the final hymn was sung. As the organ thundered 'Thine be the glory' round the church, people's hearts were uplifted. Yes indeed, where was the sting of death? Where was the victory of the grave? For as the prison officers who shouldered her coffin walked steadily down the aisle towards the open church door, a sense of resurrection and the Christian's eternal hope meant that many sad hearts were raised, catching the sense of purpose and faith with which Norma had viewed her own death.

Later Noel wrote about her funeral in the prison prayer letter:

As I write this letter so many memories are filling my mind, of years that I have shared a ministry with my wife Norma, and although she is now with the Lord she loved and served, I feel that in writing this letter, she is sharing it with me.

Thank you for the beautiful cards and letters of loving concern which many of you sent, and for the prayer support which helped me and my daughters realise that we were not alone at this time of grief. Your love has given us the impetus to pick up the pieces again. One letter from a prayer partner's dream diary read as follows: 'I saw a lovely lady dressed as a bride entering the kingdom of heaven. I was told she was Norma. And as the gates of the Beautiful City opened wide—so she went in singing, and that is where she is now—singing in praise to her Lord.'

What a wonderful encouraging vision! It reminded me of the moment when the six prison officers carried Norma's coffin out of St Paul's Church, to a full congregation singing 'Majesty'. Yes, she would have been singing the Lord's praise as she entered heaven's gate. Was it any wonder that our Governor Bill Ginn said that normally funerals depressed him, but he experienced a great uplift as he shared with the crowded church at Norma's farewell?

Over the years God has blessed Norma and myself in our ministry for his kingdom. She was the incentive and the encouragement to me in all that we did, and I miss her very much.

As a final tribute, the Rabbi from Heathlands Nursing Home led a Memorial Service for Norma on 9th July. This was very moving. Although she and he had come from differing backgrounds of faith, they had had a great respect for each other. Norma had respected the Jewish faith and was interested in it.

So a chapter was closed for the Proctor family. Noel tried to prepare himself for the future. The challenge would be great, he knew, both in living a life on his own now, and in still working at the prison with dedication. How difficult was that going to be, he wondered, now he was on his own?

Part Three
New Beginnings

Our God of the future. God assures us that after the crucifixion comes the resurrection to new life, new beginnings and new miracles. In the chaos of Strangeways stands Jesus with his arms reaching out as he says: 'Don't despair. Behold I make all things new. Heaven and earth will pass away, but the word of the Lord endures for ever.'

Praise God. So hang in there, Noel. Romans 8:28 is still *our verse*.

From Norma's note in Noel's new Bible, 1990.

16

Coming to Terms

Noel awoke and lay quietly for some moments in the double bed upstairs at home. He still went to sleep on the same side of the bed as he had always done and woke up on the same side. He did not need to reach out to the other side to feel its uncreased emptiness. In any case, he had slept there on his own for some weeks before Norma had died, when he and Susan had made her a bed-sitting room downstairs. Yet he could never get used to it: the being on his own in bed, the quietness in the house, the way everything remained exactly as he had left it the night before in the bedroom.

Oh yes, he was all right. He was warm and comfortable. His fridge was stocked with food, much of it from kind friends and neighbours. He knew he had to be thankful—there were so many visitors and phone calls and invitations that he did not have much time to be lonely. The girls were a great help and Becky was still based at home, which made a lot of difference. He sighed and turned over and looked at his watch. It said 6.45am. It was too early to get up, although soon Charlie would be whining to be let out. Then he would hear Becky begin to move as she got ready to go out to her job as a care assistant at Heathlands. It had been hard for Becky—coping with leaving college, her revision and 'A' levels as Norma was dying, and then

167

Norma's death and further 'A' levels to be taken. He turned over and looked at his watch again. At least Becky was not left in the house on her own all day while he was at work. She had the holiday job at Heathlands to occupy her mind and give a framework to her days before she went off to Edinburgh University in the autumn.

The minutes ticked on and Noel knew he ought to get up. So far Charlie had not whined, but Noel knew he would soon be making a fuss to go out into the garden. Somehow Noel was finding it harder and harder each morning to get up and face the day. He simply did not want to get out of bed in the mornings. It was hard to understand himself at times. He had always had boundless energy and a love for his work. Getting up in the morning had always been the least of his problems. Now, however, he found himself thinking of the day ahead with something akin to dread. How was he going to cope with the incessant demands at work? With always having to have a word of encouragement? With planning, looking ahead—the person who was paid to be the official believer in hope?

'Oh stop it, you idiot,' he said to himself and flung the covers back. The sun was shining round the curtains into the room, but he felt no inclination to get out of bed and draw them back. If Norma had been there, she would have welcomed such a day.

'Dad,' came Becky's voice from down the landing, and simultaneously Charlie barked.

Noel sat up and swung his legs out. He dragged himself up and reached for his dressing-gown and slippers. 'Hello,' he called to Becky as he set off downstairs. He patted Charlie, taking some comfort from the Yorkshire terrier's hairy licks and weavings round his feet. He waited in the doorway while the dog trotted round the garden, sniffing everything. The day ahead of him stretched out as a blank. There was nothing to look forward to, he thought; nothing nice could ever happen again. Everything was dreary without Norma. Charlie shot back, scattering hair as he went. Noel sighed. He knew he must not let himself think like this. He had peace in one way, because he knew that Norma was with the Lord. He knew that one day he and she would be together again. It was just the living now that was so hard. Everything in their home spoke to him about her: her clothes, her antiques, even her friends who brought round cakes and offered their help. It all underlined how terribly he missed her, how terribly empty the house was, how empty his life was.

He raised his chin a fraction. Well, Becky would be down soon and it was up to him to be a father to her and have a cup of tea with her before she went to work. As ever, her arrival in the kitchen in a frantic last-minute rush raised his spirits and even brought a smile to his face. He was late himself now and he rushed through breakfast and getting dressed. Just as he was leaving the phone rang. He grabbed it. 'Dad, it's me—Helen. Are you all right?'

'Yes, darling.' He paused a fraction. 'I'm all right. Are you?'

She said, 'Yes, not too bad.'

'I'll ring you tonight, darling.'

'OK.' Her voice sounded happier. 'Bye, Dad.'

He put the phone down. How kind his daughters were. How they were trying to mother him. Sue had been on the phone last night, planning to come over for the following weekend. He was wrong, he thought, to allow himself to imagine that there was nothing to look forward to; because the truth was that he would *always* have them to look forward to, no matter what.

He backed his car out and drove off to the prison. The lightening of his mood, however, did not last. He found himself getting tense over the wheel, and sitting hunched in the driver's seat. Why on earth was he forcing himself to go into work anyway? *I've got far more troubles than these characters I'm going to help with* their *problems and difficulties and family squabbles*, he thought. He drove too fast into a parking space and had to jam his foot on the brakes. *My problems are far greater.*

The day passed as he knew it would. He was fine while he was at the prison, but once at home again all he wanted to do was bury himself in a corner and fend off the world. When he was at home he felt as if he could not face inmates or staff the next day. Yet when he was at work such thoughts seemed unrealistic. He pulled himself up from his chair and looked at the vacuum cleaner. Suddenly, even the energy required to plug it in seemed too much. Norma had always kept the place so neat and welcoming, so, reluctantly, he changed his mind and ended up by hoovering the entire downstairs. Later he ate his tea, talked to Becky, spoke to Helen on the phone and wrote a note to Susan. Then he sat back exhausted. He had never really realised before how much Norma did, both in running the house and in mothering the girls. She had always talked to them about their futures and their careers, as well as any problems they might have. Now there was only him, and although he was more than willing to try and enter into Norma's role with them, he found it a new experience and one which required him to learn how to be the most helpful.

That night, although he felt drained and tired out, he found it hard to get to sleep. Getting up the following morning was even more difficult than the day before. *Why do I have to bother?* he thought. *My problems are overwhelming me. I'm so lonely, so tired, so fed-up.* The bedroom was empty and still and, of course, there was no Norma. There never would be any Norma again, this side of eternity. *Why on earth do I need to go and help the prisoners, when most of them have far fewer problems than I've got?* he thought again, frowning.

He went, however, just the same. He backed his car out of the drive and drove doggedly down the same old road, while his heart was entirely drained and he felt completely lonely.

Most of the men in the prison at the time were remand prisoners. There were usually under 400 of them and a lot of them were making court appearances. This meant that Noel had little opportunity to invite them to his classes, as they did not get back in time. So once he had checked who might be available for groups and classes later on in the day, he was a bit freer to visit men who were serving their sentences.

This particular morning he went to see a man called John, who had asked for a copy of the Good News Bible the week before. Noel opened his cell door and said 'hello' to John, who was sitting on the bed. The hard-backed Good News Bible lay on the bed beside him. John looked up and said straight out, 'Noel, I was praying for you last night.'

Noel's expression did not alter. He leaned his head slightly. 'Thank you,' he said.

John said, 'I know you're going through a difficult time.'

Noel looked at him properly and saw the concern on the younger man's face, the blond crew-cut, the frown marks between his eyebrows. He sighed. 'Go on, lad.' He knew John meant well.

John leaned forward. 'I asked God. I said, "God, I want you to give me a message for Noel."' He pointed to the Bible. 'But I didn't know where to look.'

Noel came and sat on the bed next to John. He

waited to hear the inevitable platitude or verse that somehow would not speak to him any more. John was busy searching through the Bible and Noel felt like saying, 'Look, if you use the Bible as a lucky dip, hunting for guidance, and you let a hard-backed version "fall open", it will nearly always fall open in the middle at Isaiah or the Psalms. It's no good treating the Bible like that. It's not a magic book. We've got to get to know our Bible and study it and learn from it in the normal way.' A joke rose to his lips about a man who asked for a message from God and opened his Bible at random three times. The first time he read, 'Judas went out and hanged himself.' The second time he read, 'Go thou and do likewise.' And the third time he read, 'What thou doest do quickly!' But somehow Noel did not feel in a jokey mood, and in any case it would only deflate John if he were to get a quick laugh, when the lad was so in earnest.

'Go on then, John,' he said at last. 'I'm listening.'

John took a deep breath and with his finger on the small print read carefully. 'Isaiah 43 verse 2.' He stopped and looked at Noel. 'I've put my own words into it, like. It seems . . . right somehow.'

Noel was silent, rebuked by John's concern. *He's only had a Bible for one week*, thought Noel. *Who am I to say God cannot give him a message when his Bible falls open?*

John read, ' "When you pass through the waters of affliction I will be with you; and when you pass through the rivers of tragedy they will not overflow you. When you go through the fire of bereavement you will not be burned, neither will heat kindle upon you, for I am with you," says the Lord.'

Noel bowed his head and sat in silence. John closed the Bible and was quiet. In a few moments Noel found he could not hold back his tears. They flowed down his cheeks. John put his arm round Noel. Together they sat for some minutes in the cell and Noel felt comforted. At last he got up and blew his nose. 'I'll come and see you later,' he managed to say and then slipped away.

When he got the chance to sort out his feelings, Noel realised that God's ways of dealing with people were truly amazing. A young inmate, not even professing to be a Christian, had helped him and ministered to him with what certainly was a direct message from God. In a strange way he felt less lonely, as if he belonged more to the human race. He no longer felt as if he were estranged from God by his grief.

In the afternoon Noel went to see John. He shook him by the hand and said simply, 'Thank you.' In the minutes that followed John talked at length and asked how he too could become a Christian. Noel found himself overjoyed to be able to lead him to a personal faith in the Lord Jesus Christ.

As they talked further John shared some of the problems and hardships of his own life and Noel tried to help him. Really, they were just like an older and a younger brother struggling amid the problems and frailties of this life to cling onto a belief in Jesus. In spite of everything, God was still there. Noel turned and looked back at John before he locked the cell door behind him, and his grin was genuine this time.

Noel clung onto this verse from Isaiah and repeated it many times to himself as the days and weeks slipped by. Yet it was a deeply difficult time and each day was a passage of time to be endured.

He found himself feeling that he too was in a prison. Whereas the men he dealt with were behind actual bars, he was in a prison within himself. He had seen this many times in other people, and now became aware that he felt the same. He realised that prisons of the mind are greater and more powerful than prisons of bricks and mortar. They need dealing with, these prisons we make for ourselves within our own personality and character. Perhaps that was why David, in the Psalms, wrote, 'Bring my soul out of prison that I may praise thy name.' Noel was comforted as he meditated on these words. He had walked with God for many years and knew that he could not give up on his faith easily or lightly. But when was he going to feel that peace and freedom within himself and so experience real freedom and joy in Jesus Christ? It was strange how he could still preach about it and mean it, in his public position, and yet all that seemed to remain for him privately was a blankness and dreariness that stretched endlessly ahead of him into the future without Norma.

Noel was to look back at this time in his life and accept that God does not make mistakes. The realisation came to him that God had, in his severe loss, been breaking Noel. Perhaps Noel needed to rediscover the faith he had had in his early Belfast days when he had learned from Billy Johnson's practical example what being a real Christian was all about. Perhaps Noel needed to get back to his roots and had to rediscover the power of the Holy Spirit in his ways of dealing with him. He was not sure, but he clung to the core of his faith, and, like Job of old, tried to trust God in the storm, in the turmoil, in the blank, in the emptiness, in the apparent lack of meaning.

One evening, as he took Charlie for his nightly stroll, Noel found himself remembering a beautiful four-year-old girl called Maria, who was the daughter of one of the young remand prisoners. Her father was in prison and her mother was a drug addict. In spite of all this the child was a delight when she came to visit her father, trotting around the visiting room in her innocence and pleasure at seeing him. The staff too were touched by her and made a fuss of her.

One day when she was at home with her mother the drug supplier called. Soon he and Maria's mother were arguing, shouting and fighting. Maria ran between them, perhaps trying to bring about peace. No one knew. As she did so the argument became ugly, and the drug supplier lashed out at the mother in a vicious kick. Maria took the full force of the blow, staggered and fell. Later she died from this attack.

Noel walked on and on until it was getting quite dark and Charlie was trailing along, having exhausted all his energy. Why was life so bitter? And yet when the prison population heard about this incident a wave of conscience had swept over them. With the father in prison and the mother in hospital, the only people left to make the funeral arrangements were Maria's grandfather and grandmother. The prisoners asked Noel to arrange a collection, which he did. Noel remembered his own amazement when many men gave their entire weekly canteen allowance, which they received to buy cigarettes, jam, sugar, sweets or whatever they liked. In the end Noel was able to take £400 to the grandparents, which paid for little Maria's funeral. What was this power of conscience that swept over them, unless it was the voice of God calling to them? It was remarkable to be a witness of this; to see how many prisoners gave and gave again, many to the Laura Davies appeal. It was rarely spoken about in society, but Noel felt it was a beautiful thing to behold the power of conscience as it stirred men. If God could speak to such men at such times, then surely he could be trusted to speak to Noel in his present loneliness?

One night Noel had a dream. He was not one to dream very much, and this made the resonance of the dream all the more powerful. In the dream he heard

Norma calling him by the familiar name she had always used for him. 'Noely,' she called. 'Noely.' When he awoke during the night her voice was still so real. There was no anguish in the dream and no sorrow, so what did it mean? As he sat up, fully awake, and thought about it, he realised that she had been trying to tell him that she was all right. Everything was well with her. He need not worry. He leaned back against the pillows, suddenly exhausted. *I can trust the Lord for her*, he thought. *It is good. All is well*. And he fell into a dreamless and refreshing sleep.

17

The Experience of Suffering

In the weeks and months following Norma's death Noel found himself questioning the faith that he had followed all his adult life. It was not that he set out to question in an intellectual way; but more, when he least expected, the questions raised themselves with powerful insistence in his mind. He could not ignore them, for they would not go away. Did God make mistakes? What was the purpose of the struggle, heartache, tears, pain, anguish, bewilderment and confusion which people experienced in this life? Was there life after death? What did life mean anyway? Had he been kidding himself all these years about the very existence of God? What was the point of preaching the gospel to others, when he was no longer sure what truth was anyway?

Noel's professionalism at work held him to his task; and also the habits of a lifetime meant he did not neglect to attend church, to meet with other believers and to read the Bible. Yet he knew something of cataclysmic proportions was shaking him to his roots and he no longer knew how to go on with God.

He still found it difficult to get up in the mornings and face the day. Often he would find himself wondering what had happened to Norma and where she had gone. He remembered how he had seen her suffer, how he had seen her flesh shrink off her so that she no longer looked like the girl he had known and the woman he had loved. He had sat at her side in the funeral parlour and looked at her, and watched her and prayed with her. Doubts had come into his mind then. Was there something on the other side? What was it all about? Where was she now?

Such thoughts gnawed away at him and he still felt as if he were in another prison—a prison within himself and a prison that was hurting him very deeply. *Who can I go to?* he thought. Everyone looked upon him as the clergyman, the preacher, the man who knew all the answers. He had to tell the men in prison that there was a better way of life, that Christians could see their loved ones on the other side, that we would have a new body, that the old things would pass away, and that there would be no more tears, pain, suffering, or death! He buried his head in his hands momentarily, then raised it and shook it as if to clear his mind. Here he was, questioning it all. What had happened to him? What on earth was going on? And how would it all end?

One day in the prison, Noel was told that a man called James had had a sudden heart attack and had been rushed to North Manchester General Hospital. He was only in the hospital for about half an hour when he had another heart attack and died. However, the medical staff were able to resuscitate him and save him. So two days later Noel went up to the hospital in order to see him. Driving over in the car Noel wondered what he would find when he got there. James had been very insistent all the time Noel had known him that the Bible was 'Hans Christian Andersen'. According to James everything in the Bible was a fairy tale; there was no point to life. You lived and you died, and that was the end of it.

Noel walked into the Coronary Care Unit and was told that James was unconscious. So Noel simply went to his bedside, took his hand and prayed for him out loud. Just as he was finishing praying, a male nurse came in and said to Noel, 'Do you think that works?'

Noel looked at him with a grin and said, 'Well, you ask him in a couple of days' time and James'll tell you!' Then Noel left.

Two more days passed by and Noel visited again. This time James was sitting up in bed, smiling all over his face. His first words were, 'Thank you, Noel, for praying for me. I heard you!'

Noel was amazed. 'You heard me?'

'Yes.'

'Well, that's incredible.' And it flashed through Noel's mind how many times people go into the presence of someone who is unconscious and assume they cannot hear. People could say tactless things like, 'She doesn't look a bit well,' or, 'I don't think he's going to make it,' and be completely unaware that the patient may be able to hear, even though they cannot respond. Hearing is apparently one of the last faculties to disappear.

'Thank you for praying for me,' said James again.

Noel was silent. Here was a man who believed the Bible was a fairy story now thanking him for praying for him!

'It's a bit like old Paddy,' said Noel, trying to make a joke out of the situation to give himself time to come to terms with it. 'When the doctor came in and examined him, he said to Paddy's wife, "I'm afraid you're not going to have him for very long," and Paddy opened his eyes and said, "I'm all right!" His wife tapped him on the arm and said, "Be quiet! The doctor knows better than you do!"'

James smiled briefly and then stared at Noel. 'Listen,

Noel,' he said. 'When I went into this experience of death I was in a place where it was so dark that it was a darkness you could feel. Everything was pressing in upon me. Away in the distance I could see a light and something within me was urging me to get to that light—to get there as quickly as I could. And so,' he continued, 'I started my journey to get to the light. I stumbled and fell in the pitch darkness. I couldn't see where I was going, but eventually I got to the light. Just as I was about to step through the doorway into the place where the light was, the door slammed in my face. And that's when they brought me back. They brought me back to life in Intensive Care.'

James looked at Noel intently, and he said, 'Noel, you know what my attitude has been in the past. But I'll tell you this. Nobody can tell me now that there's not something on the other side.'

So Noel sat and talked to James about the Lord, and about God's power. Noel knew that James did not know anything about the questioning he himself was going through at the time. James knew nothing of the doubts penetrating Noel's personality and shaking the very roots of his faith.

As Noel left the ward that day, after talking at length with James, he could not help but reflect that somehow God was deeply involved. If it was not so serious, it would be funny. Noel thought, *God, you've used that man to minister to me and he didn't even know he was doing it*. He got into his car in the hospital car park and sat there for a little while, thinking about what James had said; thinking about his own doubts, his own fears, his own misapprehensions; thinking about his own weaknesses and failings. And suddenly he just burst into tears. 'Oh Lord, you're so gracious, you're so loving. How is it that you use the things that are so outside our thoughts and imaginations to speak to us, to teach us, to bring us back to the place where we ought to be?' James' near death experience was to give Noel a new hope.

In the weeks that followed, some of the pieces of the jigsaw that had so troubled Noel's mind and heart began to settle into place. He began to understand a little of the meaning of all the sufferings he had endured over the past eighteen months. And it was not only him, but inmates, staff and family alike. Everything he had worked for in the prison had seemingly been swept away in the riot. Everything he had built his life around at home had seemingly died with Norma.

And yet . . . and yet he was beginning to realise there was a purpose in it all. It was not an easy or quick realisation, but slowly the ideas came together. He thought about a story he had read where a scientist told how he had watched insects emerging from their cocoon. Each time, a piece of horny shell appeared to hinder the insects' progress, but when the scientist tried to help one creature by removing the shell with tweezers, it curled up and died a few moments later. Then the scientist realised that the shell had a purpose: it caused the insect to develop muscles so that it could survive in the big world it was joining. Noel wondered whether perhaps human beings needed the struggle as well. Perhaps God allowed the struggle, heartache and confusion to enable them to develop those spiritual muscles so necessary if they were going to be any use for the kingdom of God. Perhaps the experience of pain and suffering drives humans back to the cross and makes them sort out their priorities in life. And if that is true, then obviously God does not make mistakes.

As Noel reflected on these things—and as he looked back over the time of the riot and its aftermath; over Norma's illness and death—he finally saw that God was breaking him, stripping away all the props in his life, making him rediscover his faith afresh. He was rediscovering the power of the Holy Spirit and his ways of dealing with people; rediscovering his own message and calling; relearning that simplest and most profound of all lessons: what it means to trust the Lord, in everything and all the time. God had been by his side all the time, even though Noel had not realised it. God had known Noel's needs and, as the old poem says so clearly, 'When there is only one set of footprints, it is then that he's carrying you.'

James' testimony to life and light 'on the other side' brought Noel back to rediscover, as it were, the Lord Jesus Christ. In turn Noel now saw that there was an urgency in his ministry and his message; that he had been helped to see that men needed to change, to be ready for that day when they were going to meet the Lord. *And I'm learning,* thought Noel, *by the experiences that God is bringing me through, by the things he is teaching me and by the way he is ministering to me, that my best is not good enough. It has to be what God wants.*

He found himself remembering a story he had read once about a man called Sir John Thornhill. He was an artist and he was asked to paint a mural in a church. The scaffolding went up and the planks on top of the scaffolding, and Sir John and his apprentice began work on the mural. When they had it completed Sir John stood back to look at his handiwork. He was so engrossed in the detail of what he had done in the painting that he forgot where he was on top of the scaffolding, and he was going further and further back. The young apprentice suddenly realised that he was near the edge of the scaffolding. If he shouted he would maybe make Sir John fall, so he did the only thing he could think of. He grabbed one of the paintbrushes, ran forward, and slapped it down the mural. Sir John dived at him. 'What are you doing,' he said, 'destroying my painting?' Then suddenly he realised that by destroying the painting, which could be repaired, the apprentice had saved his life.

Noel considered how sometimes God takes the thing that is precious to us in order to give us his best. Our own preciousness, our own belongings, our own family, our own loved ones—perhaps they become so precious to us that his best is left to one side. Sometimes it is a hard lesson to learn, and yet it is only by learning it that we can experience God's blessing.

On 9th November 1991, just over five months after Norma's death, the prison chaplaincy team organised a Prison Fellowship Rally in the Methodist Central Hall, Manchester. When the evening arrived the hall was full, many having brought coachloads from all around the North-West to hear about the chaplaincy's work in prison. Ex-prisoners and wives came, prison visitors came, ordinary churchgoers who received the prayer letter and prayed for the work came too. Folk who were simply interested to find out more came along and waited expectantly to hear what Noel was going to say.

First, however, Ross Peart, the Methodist chaplain, got up and welcomed everyone to the hall, which had been lent by his church for the occasion. He announced, to general clapping, that Noel had been made an Honorary Canon of Manchester Cathedral. So Noel got up, thanked him and stood in front of the crowd. He was wearing his dog collar as usual, and a poppy for Remembrance Sunday. 'I don't know why they've made me a canon,' he said with a grin. 'Maybe no one else would do the job! And there again,' his grin broadened, 'maybe they'll want to fire me!'

After the laughter had died down he spoke seriously for a few minutes about what had been happening in his life since Norma had died. 'I thank God for the eighteen years he gave Norma and myself to see our girls grow up and find careers. Those were eighteen bonus years.' He talked with pride about his daughters for a moment and then he paused. 'Norma used to say that as long as she had a job to do for the Lord, then she would be alive to do it. She used to wonder why others died, and she was still alive; but that was the reason. She still had a job to do. About three weeks before she died, she told me she was quite ready to go, because she knew she had completed the work on earth that God had given her to do. "I have fulfilled my job," she said, "and I am ready to go home."'

Noel leaned forward on the lectern, his face intent. The green curtains on the stage behind him were closed, hanging in folds. Only the illuminated cross stood out against them, quite stark and bright. 'How good it was in those last three weeks that we were able to talk about Norma's approaching death as a family. We tried to prepare the girls. It is so important. So important to talk and share and tell your loved ones that you love them. One night, as we shared, with Helen playing the piano, we sang "Great is thy faithfulness" and I'd like us to sing that hymn tonight.'

Noel led the singing, conducting the audience with his face alight. He radiated strength and energy and purpose. And, although he did not say it, it was apparent to some watching that God had indeed brought him very low, like Job; but now, knowing so much about heartache, hurt, loneliness and struggle, Noel was still with God, and being gently restored to that new life and phase of ministry that Norma had prophesied would happen back in February when she had been in Christie Hospital. He was like a man who has had all the stuffing completely knocked out of him; and then, ever so gently, been reassembled again. The marks of his sufferings would always be with him. But the joy and quietness of the Lord were also with him, and in a new way. He was like a man whom suffering has rinsed in mighty waters and then placed, with a surprising peace, back on the river bank.

'Since the riot,' said Noel, 'we've lost Garth Rogers, the Methodist minister, and Peter Smith, the RC priest, to other prisons. Ian Ferguson, from the Church Army, has gone to Stafford Prison. We have been joined by Brendan Curley, from the RC cathedral in Salford and he would like to share a few words about how he has settled down to a life behind bars!'

Brendan got up, looked at the audience and told them, quite simply, how he had conducted his first interview in Strangeways. 'I had to interview a man who had been remanded for committing a murder. I expected to meet a big man who was full of aggression; instead of which I met a man full of fear and insecurity. He was the father of several children and he was haunted day and night by what he had done. He could never get away from himself and had to face himself and the consequences of his action every moment of every day. I longed to say something significant to this man, something helpful. But somehow it was hard to find the words.' He paused. 'I found the whole experience quite overwhelming.

'The way the media present crime and criminals is to make the people who haven't committed crimes feel good and very self-righteous. Us and them; the good guys and the bad guys. But when I'd been at Strangeways for a few months,' said Brendan, 'I realised that many of the prisoners can be generous and thoughtful and caring. It's not a case of us and them really. I've thought a lot about the word "redemption" in these weeks and what it means; for God was in the world reconciling it to himself. Inside Strangeways is a lot of broken and suffering humanity. But,' he stopped for a few moments and looked out into the hall, 'it is frightening how some men have given themselves to violence. The violent action and reaction. Nevertheless, God has called all of us to turn to face him and to be reconciled with him and be at peace with him. All of us have done wrong of one kind or another. We all need forgiveness. We all need to be reconciled to God.'

Amid applause he sat down and Noel took over again, singing the old favourite 'Take my life and let it be, consecrated, Lord, to thee'. Again, as he sang, the strength of his renewed dedication was apparent. Even though he was unaware of it, there was a new singleness of mind, determination and purposefulness about him.

'Let me introduce Alan to you,' cried Noel and beckoned forward a very tall young man, who had to have the microphone adjusted to a new height. People settled down in their seats and waited to hear him. Alan spoke quietly and seriously. 'I was on remand for committing a serious crime. It was going to be my second sentence. Anyway, I asked if I could go to the church service one Sunday so as I could have a chat to my mate who was also on remand. During the service I wasn't really listening because I was too busy talking to my mate, but I did hear a bit. It was about a real rose and some artificial roses, and a bee coming in and finding the real rose. At the time I thought, "What on earth is Noel Proctor on about?"' He grinned and the audience responded.

'When I got back to my cell I found that I couldn't stop thinking about it all. What did Noel's talk mean? What did it mean to be real, like the real flower? I knew I could get three, five, seven years in prison. It came over me that I had wasted my life and that my life was false and artificial. People used to see me walking down the street looking smart and say, "Alan, you must be doing well." But I knew really that there was nothing behind it and that I'd perhaps only have 10p in my pocket. I asked my cell mate what he thought and he thought I was mental. He said, "Are you after Noel Proctor getting you a phone call?" Anyway,' Alan laughed, 'I said I wanted to see Noel and he came along. I said I wasn't happy in my life and he said, "Do you want the Lord Jesus in your life?" So I said, "Who is the Lord Jesus?" We talked more and I decided to say that yes I did want Jesus in my life. We prayed and nothing happened. Anyway, Noel gave me a Bible and I read a bit about Jesus Christ and I got interested, so I delved into the Bible a bit more and started going to Noel's groups. It was funny, but gradually I realised that things were changing and I wanted them to change. The pictures on the cell walls came down, and the way I dressed and made up my bed roll changed. When I was at the meetings there began to be a warmth in me and I started being happy.' He shrugged his shoulders. 'Happy in Strangeways! Then if I read about a victim of a crime in the paper sometimes I cried about them, whereas before I would think, "Good on yer, mate," about the criminal. So I told Mum and Dad.' The audience waited in anticipation. 'I think they thought I was after religion so that I could get my sentenced shortened. But at the trial they gave me three years, which was what I expected, and nothing was mentioned about my Christianity.

'I've been free for a year now. It's true that temptations do come after release and they came to me. I've failed Jesus Christ many times, but he has never failed me. Six months ago I got a job.' He paused. 'Jesus is a great man and I love him.'

He went and sat down to a round of applause. The people who were listening acknowledged his seriousness of purpose and intent. Noel stood up and said, 'When Alan came out of prison I had a phone call from a policeman who was going into schools and he said, "Is there anyone you know of who could come into schools with me and talk to the youngsters?" And I immediately thought of Alan. I gave him Alan's name. He got in touch with him and Alan was thrilled with this idea. He began to go into the schools and talk to the youngsters and tell them how he had been a bully, how he had been a tough character and how God had changed him into a new creation in Christ. The policeman rang me up about two weeks afterwards and he said, "I have taken him to three different schools, and his experience of what God has done in his life and how God has changed him is remarkable. This lad is really helping these young people." Alan has shared with us tonight and as well as that he's joined up with a church and he's going forward with Jesus.'

Noel smiled at Alan and then everyone began to sing again. The meeting was nearly over.

18

Changes of Heart

In April 1992 Noel drove to the Methodist church, Bury, to attend a wedding blessing. As he sat listening to music playing and waiting for the bride to arrive, Noel could see the back of the bridegroom's head at the front of the church. Noel got up and went over to shake him by the hand. 'Hello, young man!' he said and Will turned round, his face lighting up. 'Hello, Noel!' The two men grasped each other's hands fervently and Noel slipped back to his seat. It was inevitable that his thoughts should turn to Norma and his own wedding in 1964 and there was an element of sadness in his memories. Yet, resolutely, Noel put this on one side. Today was Will and Margaret's day; she was remarrying and now being blessed in that marriage to a man she had divorced four years previously.

Noel remembered Will on the day of the riot in Strangeways' chapel. He had helped to rescue the prison officer and, as a result, had had his sentence shortened eventually. He was also the inmate who had later cleaned up his cell to the amazement of the policeman on duty in Leamington Spa.

Now, as the moments ticked by and the guests in the church waited for Will's bride to arrive, Noel thought about the transforming power of Jesus Christ.

Will had been a £1,000-a-week drug addict. He had

been a notorious thug in the town, needing to get the money by any means to pay for his heroin addiction. He was so addicted and difficult to live with that in the end his wife Margaret divorced him, and he was left without her and his son and daughter. He was caught out trying to get away with a serious fraud and was remanded in custody at Strangeways.

Noel remembered clearly how Will used to speak about this time in his life, and he smiled to himself. 'I kept noticing this singing and whistling nutter who used to walk round the landings. I asked my cell mate who it was and he said, "Oh, that's Noel Proctor. If you want a phone call, he's a soft touch. He'll get you one."' So Will thought about this and decided to ask Noel to ring his wife for him and find out why she had not been to see him. When Noel returned from making the call his face was serious and he tackled Will about it straight away.

'You are separated,' he said.

'Er, yes.'

'I've found out from your wife that you've done a lot to hurt her. You've broken into her home twice to get money to pay for your addiction. And you've burgled your brother as well!' Noel's voice had risen with amazement.

Will bit his lip. He knew in his heart how low he had sunk and hated himself for it. He waited for Noel to tell him off, but instead Noel said, 'I think I can give you a Bible if you'd like one.'

Will frowned. He did not want to offend Noel and so he replied, 'Yes. Thank you,' even though he knew he would not be bothered to read it.

Noel said, 'You have hurt your ex-wife a lot and you are going to have to give her time to get over this burglary.'

'I know,' muttered Will.

After Noel had gone Will looked at the Bible in his hands. As a boy in Bury he had gone to church, been in the Sunday school and the choir, but now it meant nothing to him. He got up, the Bible still in his hands. He looked around for somewhere to put it. There was nowhere, so casually he chucked it into the corner of the cell. There it lay, title upwards, behind a chair.

When his cell mate noticed the Bible he said to Will, 'Hey, have you read Noel Proctor's book?'

'What?'

'It's called *The Cross Behind Bars*. It's supposed to be all right.'

Will shook his head. But the following Monday, when he was allowed to go on his weekly visit to the library for some Westerns, the first thing he saw was *The Cross Behind Bars* on the shelf. It seemed to jump out of the shelf at him, so, with a quick glance around, he took it down and hid it in his pocket. Then he got his allocation of paperbacks about cowboys and strolled back to his cell, untroubled by the fact that he had stolen a book.

As he read Noel's story, Will became gripped. He read it three times in all, and the only part of it he was to recall afterwards was the incident when a lifer at Dartmoor asked the local bishop if there was a sin God could not forgive. The bishop replied, 'The only sin God cannot forgive is the unconfessed sin.' This thought would not leave Will alone. He started to borrow all the books he could find from the chaplains' library and read them carefully. In the end he got tired of reading about how men and women in prison found this guy they called Jesus. Will had no intention of giving up his macho image during the day, especially in front of his cell mate, but at night, as he lay trying to get to sleep on his bunk, all the pressures and the guilt crowded in on him. He knew how deeply he had hurt Margaret and his children. And what about his parents? And his brother? All the things he knew he had done wrong, and all the people he had wronged, crowded into his mind.

He enjoyed reading and so asked another prisoner if he had any books to lend him. The prisoner handed him a book with its back cover ripped off. The front cover was entitled *Holes in Time*. It was the autobiography of a gangster. Will grinned. Now this looked all right. It would be a good read, pass the time, and obviously would not be religious. So he settled down on his bunk to read. Halfway through he was startled to read that the author, Frank Constantino, had given his life to Jesus Christ and decided to become a modern disciple.

Will put the book down and stared at the ceiling in the cell. Was there nowhere, and no book, where he could get away from this guy, Jesus Christ? He waited all day, but there was no opportunity to be alone. At night he somehow found he could not pray in front of his cell mate.

Next morning Will asked his mate to slop out. 'I did it yesterday!' said the cell mate. 'It's you today.'

'Oh, go on. Please. I'll do it tomorrow.'

'Oh, OK,' said the cell mate, grumbling a little.

Will waited until he had gone with the bucket. As soon as the cell door banged shut, he buried his head in his hands. Could he do it? All he remembered from Frank Constantino's book was he had written that for good or bad he could not undo what he had done in the past. All there was left was for him to go forward and start a new life. But could Will do this? Could he start a new life? Three times he had tried to come off drugs and each time was bitter. *I can't face that again*, he thought. Even though he was free of them now, he guessed he'd go straight back onto them again once he got out of prison. He picked up the Bible from the corner and looked at it. His cell mate would be coming back soon. *All right*, he decided suddenly, *I'll do it. I'll ask Jesus Christ into my life as well.* After a few moments he opened his eyes. For a second he wondered where he was. Then of course, where else could he be but in a cell at Strangeways, on remand? Did he expect Jesus to wave a magic wand? He got up and looked at his face in the mirror—but it was still the same, the same old Will Michaels, who looked no different now that he had asked Jesus into his life. The memory of all his past behaviour swept into his mind and he cried out, 'Oh, forgive me. Forgive me. Please forgive me.' There was a clattering outside the cell door and a laugh. His cell mate was back, empty bucket swinging. Will sat on his bunk again and composed his face. 'Hiya, mate,' he said as the other man walked into the cell.

When he awoke the following morning Will found he felt a lot better. He could only describe it to himself as feeling free.

'Hey!' he called out to his mate. 'Hey, I'm free! I'm a new creation in Christ, even though I don't deserve it!'

'Oh, shut it!' said the other man. 'I don't want to know!'

For the next fortnight Will immersed himself in the Bible. He joined some of Noel's groups, and told as many inmates as he could about his new-found faith. He got a lot of taunts for this, but quite a few other lads began to take notice of him and listen to him. He began to find it difficult to cope with all the different things people were saying to him and as he prayed he realised that he needed a sign. He needed God to indicate to him one way or the other that he was doing the right thing in becoming a Christian and witnessing to his newly found faith. It just seemed to come into his mind that he should write a letter to the author of *Holes in Time* and maybe in the reply the author would say something that would be a part of that sign.

One evening, about midnight, he decided he would write to Frank Constantino and tell him what had happened. So next morning he asked his cell mate to help him write the letter. 'Can I write abroad from prison?' he asked.

'It's fourteen years since I was in before, and I can't remember the rules,' his mate groaned. 'Are you a nutter or something?' he asked.

However, he did try to help Will work out the best way to write the letter. It so happened that Noel called in later to see how he was, so Will asked him straight out if he would help them with the letter. Noel stood quite still and stared at the two of them. 'You don't know what God is doing for you, do you?' he said. 'I'll have to pray for you. Come here, the both of you!'

Will never took in the prayer. He was too busy trying to pray his own. When Noel had finished, Will opened his eyes and noticed his mate trying to conceal the fact that he was brushing away a tear from his eye. *It's no good worrying about your macho image when you're really getting to grips with Jesus*, thought Will kindly.

Noel interrupted his thoughts. 'Didn't you hear what I was praying, man?'

Will stared at him blankly. 'Er, sorry. I, er, wasn't listening.'

Noel sighed in exasperation. 'You don't need to send that letter!'

Will's face fell. Perhaps he and his mate had got it wrong, had . . .

'Because Frank Constantino is coming in person, in three weeks' time, to this prison, all the way from America. So you can hand it to him personally!'

At Will's trial he was given four years for fraud. After becoming a Christian he decided to confess to the police the three further crimes of burgling Margaret twice and his brother once, and he was given a further six months for these crimes.

After he had been released some time, the police in Bury asked him to accompany them into schools and tell the young teenagers how and why he had kicked the habit and warn them against a life of crime. Eventually his changed lifestyle won back the heart of his former wife, in spite of everything she had gone through in the past, and she agreed to marry him again. In the autumn he was going to leave his job as a lorry driver and breakdown truck driver on the motorway and do some training in the Scriptures and evangelism at Cliff College.

As Noel waited in the Methodist church that morning, he bowed his head and marvelled at the grace of God. True, it would not necessarily be easy for Will and Margaret. But with the love and power of God to help them, they would have every opportunity to make a good and stable marriage. Noel knew that the many prayer partners and churches they represented would help to pay Will's fees at college. People might knock the church—and sometimes they were right to do so—but where else in society would a man like Will find help and acceptance in his struggle to rehabilitate himself?

There was a bustle at the church door and Margaret appeared, looking radiant and carrying a bouquet. Their six-year-old daughter Patricia was a bridesmaid and their nine-year-old son Paul was an usher. Noel smiled at her and then looked over to Will; he had moved into position to greet his bride.

And to crown it all, he had chosen a former policeman to be his best man! As Will often said, the worst prisons were those you made yourself. Prisons of bricks and mortar were not as bad as those. And here was a wonderful moment in his life, when all prisons both inside and outside were being left behind.

As the year wore on Noel began to see new problems emerging in the prison. There were many changes now being implemented after the Woolf Enquiry, but the shock waves of the riot and siege still lingered on. A human price among inmates and staff alike, in terms of stress and uncertainty, was still being paid. One officer had a heart attack two years after the riot and this was put down to the stress and strain resulting from the riot. There was much uncertainty about the future as the prison had to be submitted for market testing. No one quite knew what the future would hold in terms of jobs and opportunities.

Noel and the chaplaincy team had found that being Christians did not in any way exempt them from trouble, tragedy and hurt. The general lack of certainty about the future hit them as much as it did anyone else. Noel realised, as he looked back, that he had had to learn to adapt to frequent changes as he moved through crisis, tragedy and bereavement. It wasn't easy, especially when some days he still felt like packing it all in and Norma, who had always encouraged him to keep going, was no longer at his side. Yet as he weathered these storms Noel realised that even as he had questioned the fundamentals, he had rediscovered his faith in Jesus Christ as Lord and had, as a result, an even clearer focus on what he wanted to do.

The chaplaincy team had become even more ecumenical. It was running sixteen classes a week now, with fewer than 400 prisoners in the prison. This meant that as the classes were all wing-based, they were bringing in helpers to run them, and the team was touching far more men's lives than it had ever done before. The team got a lot of help from Prison Fellowship members, from church people who had become interested through reading the prayer letter and from prison visitors who found they no longer had the number of inmates to visit (because the prison population was so much lower at that time in the smaller, refurbished building) and so wanted to come in and help with running the groups.

The prison now prepared to put in a bid under the new government rules about market testing. This was based on the continuation of the implementation of recommendations in the Woolf Report. From the chaplaincy point of view Noel felt all these were healthy developments. The chaplains would still be needed; they had the time to go and sit with prisoners who had heard bad news from home. Drugs and alcohol were the main addictions manifested by the prisoners and so teamwork was built up in counselling and group therapy skills.

A group of staff were now allocated to run each wing. This meant that staff had the opportunity to build up relationships with the inmates. Whereas in the past an officer could be on 'A' wing one day, at court the next day, and on another wing the following day, now he was able to get to know inmates on his particular wing. This relaxing of the regime, which included the fact that hats were no longer worn by the officers, meant that a real communication could grow between staff and prisoners, and in time confrontations and 'scenes' were less likely to occur.

More organisations were also offering help for rehabilitation of offenders after they left prison: Lydia House, the Adullam Homes, the New Life Centre in Stockport and the Langley House Trust. Joe Whelan is a field officer for the Langley House Trust. He comes into Strangeways each week and talks regularly to the men about what they are going to do when they get out, particularly if they have had problems with drugs or alcohol. The trust has hostels and homes for rehabilitation and also places for men with nowhere to go. Joe often waits for a man outside the prison on the day of his release and becomes a 'bridge' for the ex-offender. Instead of the discharge grant going straight to the man's old drug supplier or local pub, Joe helps the man and accompanies him to a hostel or a home.

Joe too served a long sentence in prison. However, he became a committed Christian during his imprisonment and since his release over ten years ago, has not reoffended. He is now welcomed by the authorities, not only in Strangeways, but also in other North-West prisons. He has proved himself to be a reliable, caring and effective field officer.

Noel found himself developing a bond with Joe, who was a great support to him after Norma died. Like a brother, Joe would insist on Noel sharing how he felt during his bereavement. This helped Noel considerably as he readjusted to life without her.

Noel began to receive more and more invitations to speak to outside organisations: many schools around Manchester, and in Cumbria; Harrow School; Magistrates groups; theological lectures in colleges; the Development Course for chaplains, and annual meetings of the Prison Service Christian Fellowship. Students from theological colleges also came into the prison to learn from the work of the chaplaincy team.

After working for over twenty years in British prisons and longing to see change, Noel felt that one positive result from the riot was that the Woolf Report recommended changes, and Strangeways was determined to put these into practice. Hope in the future era was at last rekindled.

As he thought back to 1st April 1990 when the riot had broken out in the chapel, Noel remembered that no one had ever thought that the siege would go as far as it did. Manchester had had problems, but had always contained them in the past.

The Woolf Report had brought about changes, with better sanitation, better food, more time spent out of cells, and the introduction of personal officers. Yet prison will never be an easy place. Society will make sure of that. For some prisoners being away from their families is a punishment in itself. For others, it is sadly a blessing, when they can at last get on their own, face themselves and try to make themselves a future.

19

Righteousness Delivers from Death

As Noel sat in his office one day the phone rang. When he picked it up he heard the voice of Wilfred, an ex-inmate who had recently been discharged. 'Hello there,' said Noel. 'How are you?'

'I'm fine.'

'What can I do for you?'

There was a pause. Then Wilfred said, 'Look, I've got a flat in Blackley.'

'Oh, I thought you had paid a lease on a house.'

'Well,' said Wilfred, 'what a mess that was. It's frightening what can happen once you leave prison, Noel.'

Noel agreed. He knew from hard experience with the men over the years how vulnerable they were when they first got outside.

'I'd paid my lease all through my sentence,' said Wilfred, 'just so that I *would* have somewhere to go when I got out. As soon as I arrived there the bailiff arrived and asked me to leave. When I asked him why, he said the owner had not paid the mortgage and it was going to be repossessed! So I got this flat in Blackley, but . . .'

'Go on,' said Noel.

'But somehow, Noel, I can't find a church. I can't

settle down and frankly I don't know what I am going to do if I don't find somewhere soon and settle down.'

'Have you tried your local Church of England?'

There was a pause. 'Where is it?'

'In Crab Lane. Look, I think you'll find you'll be accepted there straight away.'

'Do you think so?'

Noel laughed. 'I'm sure so,' he said and put the phone down. He sat back in his chair and thought about Wilfred.

It had still been the old Strangeways when Wilfred arrived in Reception, over six feet tall, a Forces background, divorced and very articulate. He was also cynical and not always easy to get along with. Noel grinned to himself as he recalled Wilfred's story. There he was, in Reception, over fifty years old and wondering what he had come to. All at once a rather smelly youth wandered in and sat down and put his feet up on the table. Wilfred noticed he had holes in both soles. The youth, who seemed to think he owned the place, said, 'What are you in for?'

Wilfred replied: 'Well, we won't go into that now, but what are you in for?'

The feet jigged about a bit and the youth smirked. 'I robbed a bank of £56,000!'

Wilfred could not help replying, 'Well, it's a pity you didn't buy yourself a new pair of shoes!' However, his humour was short-lived. He was given some food but the door was locked, and it seemed to Wilfred that he had to eat his dinner in a cage.

Later, he was interviewed by a member of the chaplaincy team. He answered all the questions readily enough until the minister said to him, 'Will today's decision make any difference to you 100 years from now?'

Wilfred stared. 'Are you mad? I'll be dead then anyway.'

The minister smiled and got up to go. 'You think about it,' he said.

Wilfred was put in a cell, eight by ten, on his own. It was dingy and dismal. After the door had been clanked shut and the key turned, he sat quite still on the bunk, and quite alone. He tried the door, but of course it was useless. He realised that he felt afraid, given up by everyone, and no one was left who wanted to know him. *I've led a bad life*, he thought, *since leaving the Forces when I was thirty. I was fine until then. But since* . . . He shook his head. He knew no one would accept him now or in the future, and he could hardly blame them. He got up, stretched and paced up and down. He was frightened to death, big as he was. He thought, *What am I doing here? What's my life all about anyway? I was brought up decently, and now look at me! Here I am, over fifty years old, and stuck in a cell in Strangeways*. He slumped down on the bed. He had been a good con man, he knew that. He had cheated people and robbed banks, not with a gun, but with a pen. He had found it easy, enjoyable even, to rip people off. There were people, he knew, who would never trust him again in his home town. Yet now he felt his own inadequacy and loneliness keenly.

His domestic life was a mess. He knew only too well that no one would visit him or write to him, and that there was no one else to blame but himself. And so Wilfred sat on, in the bitterness of his spirit, facing up to some very unpleasant realities while his whole world fell apart around him. What was he going to do?

As he sat on he became aware of some singing. The music was rich and stirring and reminded him of his youth in church and Sunday school. Whoever would be singing in a place like this? The music ebbed and flowed and Wilfred's heart lifted as he heard it. *It's beautiful*, he thought, and wondered what it all meant. Later he realised that the central rotunda in the prison, topped by a dome, had excellent acoustics and that was why the music had sounded so wonderful as it floated down the wings.

Next morning he said to the man in the cell next door as they queued to slop out, 'What was all that going on upstairs last night?'

'What?'

'The singing.'

The man chuckled. 'Oh! That's the God squad. It's the Jesus freaks, Noel's army!'

Wilfred was nonplussed. 'What do you mean? Who is this Noel?'

'Oh, he's the little bloke who runs round the landings at high speed, handing out anti-swearing tablets.'

Wilfred laughed. 'Go on!'

'You'll bump into him sooner or later. He carries packets of peppermints and calls them anti-swearing tablets!'

Mmm, thought Wilfred. *What a good idea. If your mouth gets refreshed by a mint you might not feel so inclined to give out a mouthful.* 'How do I meet this Noel?' he asked.

The man moved towards the toilets with his bucket at his side. He thought for a moment. 'Well, he plays the trumpet on Christmas Day.'

'Christmas Day! It's only June now. I can't wait til then!'

'Well, when they serve out tea you'll sometimes see him in a corner, near the centre stage where they serve out the food.'

'Right,' said Wilfred, determined to speak to Noel as soon as he could.

Later on, at tea time, Wilfred saw a clergyman

standing in the background, near the food. 'Is that him?' he asked his mate from the morning. The man nodded. So Wilfred approached Noel, wondering quite what to say. 'Er, excuse me. This singing lark, this song squad you have on a Friday—is there a chance for me?'

Noel stared straight at Wilfred and raised his eyebrows slightly. 'I don't know about that, Wilfred.'

Wilfred opened his mouth and then closed it again. He was shaken to realise that Noel knew his name. He had hardly been in the place five minutes, so how did Noel know?

'What are the chances of me joining one of your groups?' he asked, looking down at Noel from his greater height. This seemed to make no difference whatsoever to Noel, who stood his ground quite calmly.

'I don't think so at the moment. You are cynical and you'll be a disruptive element in my class.' And with that, Noel turned and walked away.

Wilfred was not happy over the next couple of days. His conscience kept bothering him and he could not get away from it, or from himself. One night he dreamed he had died and gone to hell. There were red-hot coals and he had bare feet and was afraid, and all around him hung dead rats and snakes. It was so vivid and so horrible that he woke up in a sweat and it took some time to calm himself down. He decided he must get a better life, but what could he do? He buried his head in his hands. *Just look at me*, he thought. *I am awful. And whatever is going to happen to me if I die in here?* He knew he had to do something to change himself; to be honest and decent; to get away from his conscience which was killing him. He never ever wanted to live the way he used to before he came to prison. He knew he could go back to earning his living dishonestly, but every part of him revolted against going back to that kind of life again when he was eventually released.

Two days later his cell door was flung open and Noel handed Wilfred a Bible and said, 'Read the Gospel of St John!' Then he turned and walked out again, locking the door behind him. Wilfred had hardly managed to get to his feet before the door slammed and Noel was gone. He turned the Bible over in his hand, looked at the cover carefully and then placed it by his bed.

Wilfred was not approached by Noel again until a week later. During that week Wilfred found himself wrestling day and night with the questions that haunted him: What did his life mean? And how could he ensure he would be able to live a decent and honest life when he finally got out?

On Friday evening, the following week, there was an unexpected jangle of a key turning in his cell door. The cell door flung open and a big officer was standing on the threshold. 'Jones!'

Wilfred stood up and nodded.

The officer jerked his thumb in the direction of the landing behind him. 'God squad!'

Wilfred stood a moment and then said, 'Where do I go?'

The officer nodded in the direction and said, 'Go down there and report to the lad waiting there.'

So Wilfred went along to the class, enjoyed singing and joined in the discussion. However, halfway through he caught Noel's eye and then turned away. He had started to get cynical again during the discussion and knew he should not have made that obnoxious remark that had risen, unbidden, to his lips. Afterwards he apologised to Noel.

Once back in his cell Wilfred could not settle down. Why was it so typical of him to be nasty and cynical when he really liked and admired what Noel and the other lads were doing in the meeting? He simply did not know. But he realised with a fresh force that he had to change. He must change. He must become decent again. There must be something better in life than this cell.

Finally he got undressed and settled himself to sleep, feeling terrible all the while, trapped, useless and nasty. He awoke in the middle of the night, and found that tears were falling down his cheeks. He remembered his dream of hell and was deeply disturbed. He clambered out of his bunk and walked up and down. He picked up a book he had been reading, but one glance was sufficient to tell him that for the moment it would not satisfy him in the turmoil he was in. Then his eye fell on the Bible, still closed and lying neatly where he had placed it when Noel had given it to him. With a sudden decisiveness he took two paces across the floor, picked it up and let it fall open in his hands. Then he sat on the bunk and began to read. 'Book of Proverbs' said the title, so Wilfred flipped back the pages until he found the beginning. Then he settled down to read it.

He read the entire book, all thirty-one chapters, right through. Finally he finished reading, and with the Bible still open on his knee, sat and stared unseeingly at the cell wall opposite. Every inch of his body was shaken by what he had read. Over and over and over again he could see himself in the pages. It was almost frightening, but this was a different fear from the fear he had felt when he was first locked in his cell. Slowly he turned the pages back to chapter 10 and reread the words in verse 2 that had so jumped out of the page at him when he first took them in:

> Ill-gotten treasures are of no value
> But righteousness delivers from death.

He read these words until he knew them by heart. In their stark simplicity they spoke to him, told him what he was and gave him the answers to all his questions.

Had he not spent twenty years getting 'ill-gotten treasures' by fraud and deception, only to find now that all that money was of no value to you when your world fell apart? And was he not so terrified of death that he was desperate to do anything to find an answer? And was the answer not written here in black and white, that righteousness was the key? He nodded and thought. The last thing he was was righteous, and he wanted to be righteous; to live a life doing right, saying right, following what was right. But how was he to get righteousness? He fell asleep again with this thought uppermost in his mind, and the dream and his tears were forgotten.

Next day he asked to see Noel and explained his dilemma. Noel smiled at him and said quite forcefully, 'Look at you. Don't you realise? It's God talking to you through these proverbs.'

Wilfred felt quite surprised. 'But how can God talk to me? My conscience is killing me.'

'Man is a trinity, like God is,' said Noel. 'You are spirit, soul and body.' He gestured to the cell window. 'People out there might not forgive you, but God will and can and does.'

'How?' asked Wilfred.

'Have you asked him? Have you read John's Gospel? Have you met Jesus in the gospel?'

'Er . . . no, not yet,' said Wilfred anxiously.

'Well, you get stuck into it and I'll come and see you again,' said Noel.

Wilfred read and read again. Finally, on his own, he thought to himself, *I don't follow all of it, but surely the answer must be Jesus Christ. I must accept him and his ways.* And quite quietly and soberly, he did.

It was only after he made this decision that Wilfred suddenly realised something had happened, as if somewhere deep inside him had been released. Emotions he had not experienced for years, and which he later realised were joy and happiness, began to bubble up inside him. He felt free. In the days that followed he was fully aware of the paradox of his situation. He knew he was free and released inwardly, even though outwardly he was locked in a cell, had no freedom and certainly would not be released for some time.

The curious thing was that, as Wilfred said later, he actually enjoyed being in Strangeways for all the time he served there. He had such inner peace. All his guilt went, and the loneliness which had so frightened him, no longer troubled him. He knew that if he had God, he could never be lonely. He was no longer separated from him, so he could never be lonely.

After his initial problems on release Wilfred settled happily at the church in Crab Lane and made several friends. He has kept clear of all trouble ever since. He was thrilled to be accepted by this church and became friendly with a seventeen-year-old boy there who had injured his knee. Wilfred visited the family and tried to help them. Some two years later he married the boy's widowed mother and eventually they led a church house group together, where Wilfred's practical knowledge of the Bible was put to good use.

In November 1992 he shared a platform with Noel at the Prison Fellowship Rally. Jokingly Noel introduced him. 'Wilfred used to work in the prison kitchen and dished out the sugar for the tea line. One day I said to him, "Wouldn't it be wonderful if we shared a platform together sometime?" And this is exactly what we have done many times.' Wilfred told the audience how shocked he had been to hear about the Strangeways riot when he switched on his radio one day in his flat. He had felt quite sure Noel would be all right, because, as he said, 'Noel was well loved.' Strangeways had a reputation in Manchester for being a hard place.

But nothing like the riot had ever happened before. Strangeways had never been like that. 'It was shocking,' said Wilfred, 'that Noel was treated the way he was in the riot.' He smiled at the audience and talked to them and then ended up by saying, 'Noel told me I only needed to find the right girl. I'd been a terrible husband before, but now here he was encouraging me. Anyway, I did meet the right girl and we got married. She's sitting here in the audience tonight.' The audience clapped and Wilfred said, 'I'm a difficult man to live with. But I'm not so pompous or bombastic now, although my wife might disagree!' Everyone laughed. 'We've both been ill, and I've had a stroke and I know that the Lord is saying to slow down. But I am happy. I've got a home, and a wife, and our pets; and I am happy. My present life is so good!' And amid clapping he went and sat down.

20

Looking to the Future

Life continued for everyone in the prison. Strangeways put in a bid to the Prison Department at the Home Office, to continue running the prison as they were already doing. Eventually, after a lot of uncertainty and stress about the future, this bid was accepted. The building continued to be renewed: cream paint was everywhere, the place was cleaner and lighter, the landings, stairs and wings were all made with grills or bars and this meant a physically clearer vision for everyone concerned with the running of the prison. There was a new gym, a new hospital, a new chapel and a whole new entrance area, done in red brick and toning in well with the old building. The remand section had never really closed. By March 1994 the newly refurbished Manchester prison was reopened, the five wings occupied and the number of inmates slowly built up at the rate of fifty prisoners a week, until the total of just under 900 men was reached. Sanitation was much improved: each man now has his own cell, with a toilet and washbasin either inside or adjacent to the cell. Slopping out, with all its indignities, is a thing of the past. The new kitchen facilities have also brought improvements: food is now served hot, is on the whole improved in variety and quality, and served at normal times when people outside would also be eating. The old routine of lunch at 11.30am and tea at 4.30pm has gone. Now men can make their own drinks as well.

This new element of dignity for the prisoners in their daily routine has become an incentive to them to enter into the new *compact* being requested of them by the prison authorities. In this the authorities promise to give them a purpose while they are in prison, will endeavour to help them with their problems while in prison, and will prepare them for release after prison. In return, the prisoners promise to behave themselves, go to work, and begin to look at their own lives through discussion and acceptance of help. Both parties then sign the compact, which undergirds the whole building up of the new era in the prison. Relationships between all concerned are now seen as playing a key role in the new Manchester prison.

A *personal officer* is appointed for each eight to ten inmates. He can get to know them as individuals and take an interest in them. The prisoner can choose to go to him if he needs help with any problem. In certain cases this has given great encouragement. There are still some problems, but these are becoming fewer.

Then there is *sentence planning*: during his sentence a man is given some education, he can work in the packing workshops, and if possible he is given an opportunity to learn a trade. Prisoners can learn computer skills, refurbish NHS wheelchairs, be trained and then make three-piece suites. New ideas include a hairdressing salon in the prison and special courses in painting, decorating and plastering. All this is useful employment.

There is now *pre-release* preparation. Some inmates are able to go out into one of the Christian after-care homes. If a man suffers from a drink or drug addiction, help is given both in treatment inside and also after he is released, when he can go to a special home where training and help are given to overcome his addiction. A *Job Club* has opened in prison, so men can write out to firms and industries, trying to find employment upon release. So far the results have been encouraging. Many men who have come to the Job Club have been interviewed by firms, and some have been successful and have been offered a job upon release.

The personal officer can also bring in a trained *listener* to get alongside any of his men who are finding life hard-going. These listeners are other inmates, trained to listen and absorb emotional and verbal outpourings. They can often offer support as they too will have experienced many of the same anxieties and feelings.

Telephones are now available and men can keep in touch with their wives and families, or girlfriends. This is important as it allows for continuity and openness in family relationships. In the past all this had to be done by letter. Visiting facilities have also improved. There are crèches, and inmates can have weekly rather than, as in the past, monthly visits. Men on remand can receive daily visits. This all helps to keep family relationships sound during a sentence and, hopefully, upon release.

The compact does put some demands and restrictions on the prisoners. They have to be prepared to take the right attitude towards it, learn more about themselves and their motivations. They have to want to improve. Some men have signed the compact and then thought they could stay in bed in the mornings. This is not acceptable. If they do not bother to come out to work they do not receive any pay and they are locked up again. They must accept the fact that they are to make an effort to help themselves and enter into the activities laid on by the Education Department, physical training instructors, Probation Service and chaplaincy team; all of whom are endeavouring to make structured activities available.

The chaplaincy offers Bible and confirmation classes, prayer and fellowship groups, as well as services on Sundays and a Sunday afternoon concert. Noel is finding that men come to these concerts now, not simply to get out of their cells as in the old days, but because they want to come. Such men are often very interested to find out more about an alternative to a life of crime. Noel wrote in his prayer letter:

> We have a group of inmates who have accepted Jesus, and they meet with us each morning to pray for the prison (those who live in it, and those who work in it). This is a real source of strength. David Palmer, our new assistant chaplain, who has been working for three years already with the Board of Social Responsibility regarding drug addiction in the Diocese of Manchester, has begun a drug rehabilitation group in the prison, which is being used to help men leave an addiction which will destroy them and shows them how to get really 'high' on Jesus! There is a new wave of optimism in the prison and everyone concerned is looking forward to a future, when conditions are so much improved.

When Manchester Prison came through the 1990 tragedy, Noel and his colleagues often wondered what would happen in the years that lay ahead. Now they know they are seeing developments which are useful, practical and fruitful. Naturally, it has not been easy for prison staff to readjust to the new prison and yet they are doing it. *Care teams* have now been started in every prison so that if there is any incident, such as violence or the discovery of someone who has committed suicide or whatever it may be, a team member is available to draw alongside their colleague and offer support and encouragement. Everyone knows how difficult it is to cope with the aftermath of emotions and reactions caused by such incidents; it has an effect upon staff and their families.

As Noel looks at the new Manchester Prison now he can see, as was said after the tragedies of 1990, that the phoenix is beginning to rise again from the ashes of the past. In many ways Manchester is a flagship for other big, local prisons, where men can be treated with some dignity and, above all, where men can find some sort of purpose in life. They do not have to live in the shadowland of drugs and drink. The desire of the new Manchester is to show men that there is indeed light through prison bars.

The Governor, Robin Halward, sees this as a challenge:

It is almost inevitable from time to time that you get disorder in prisons, so you construct buildings that reduce the effect of disorder as much as possible. Now we have buildings which are much stronger and much better controlled, where it will be easier to prevent any disturbance from spreading than it was in the old Strangeways.

The physical treatment of prisoners is very important. Every cell now has a toilet and a washbasin, and therefore we no longer have the degrading process of slopping out. But in the end behaviour is more about relationships than about buildings, important though they are. With the new Strangeways the emphasis is on the relationships between staff and prisoners, prisoners and prisoners, and staff and staff. This has the potential to create a community that does not have within it the seeds of destruction that existed previously.

Noel agreed with the Governor. He stood in the new chapel, so beautifully replacing the old, and was deeply thankful for all that gave hope in the new Strangeways. The chapel is smaller, of course, and men are now frisked before attending a service or group as a matter of common practice. But it is a place filled with peace and a sense of the presence of the Holy Spirit. The area is multi-purpose. The communion rail and altar dais can be curtained off, the chairs turned and the room used for films, lectures, concerts or education. But as a chapel it is as lovely as any church in the land.

Noel crossed over the blue carpet and looked at the statue of the risen Christ hanging on the wall above the communion table. The arms were outstretched towards the people, the robes flowing. The old statue and cross had been destroyed in the fire during the riot. Norma and her friends from St Paul's Church, Kersal Moor in Salford, had given money to a fund they had begun and raised the £700 needed to replace it. Then they had gone out and bought this new one and donated it to the prison chapel. Noel looked at it now, with the tiny plaque underneath in memory of his beloved Norma.

In spite of Norma's early death Noel still believes in God's healing power today. He knows that even while Norma led meetings with him and talked and demonstrated God's healing power to others she was aware that she was dying slowly of the recurrence of cancer. But she had done this out of conviction that not only was God calling her to do it, but also that in the end the healing, wholeness and salvation of the inner man were even more important than the body's physical healing. To free people from the prisons of fear, insecurity, hurt, grief and guilt was the reason why Christ himself came to the world and bore the sins of the world on his shoulders by hanging on a tree and then rising from the dead on Easter Day.

At home Noel can see Norma's vision for their parish church gradually being fulfilled. Her picture of St Paul's, Kersal Moor, being like a 'stately and colourful galleon filled with church members pulling in people sinking beneath the waves all around them' is evident both in the church's present experiences and future plans. After his retirement in the winter of 1995 ideas are being shared for Noel to base himself at this church and, with a team of church members, become involved with helping parishes in need.

Now in the chapel he bowed his head for a few moments and remained quite still in front of the statue of the risen Christ. He remembered the previous spring when he had travelled to Buckingham Palace to receive the MBE. It was on the way home in the train that he had settled down in his seat, relaxed and begun to reflect upon all the turbulent events in these last few years of his life. Gradually everything had settled into a pattern in his mind. He had come to a new understanding, an acceptance, a sense of peace. He lingered on in the chapel for a few moments; then he turned, walked quietly back across the carpet, out through the door and away into the prison.

Epilogue

Buckingham Palace—9th March 1993

Noel walked up the steps into Buckingham Palace on this special day with Helen and Becky beside him. When they reached the top of the steps Noel had to go in through one door and his daughters went inside by a different entrance. They would be shown to the visitors' seats, while he was taken to a different room and shown, along with all the other people who were to receive Honours, what he had to do, and how to do it; when to step forward, what to say, and when to step back. It was like a rehearsal, all very professional and very well done. Once inside he found himself looking around at the wonderful portraits and pictures in the corridors. It seemed quite awesome to be in such surroundings, in among such people. Noel raised his chin slightly. *What am I doing here?* he thought, as he glanced at all the others gleaming in their best clothes. He looked down at his own suit which he had hired for the day. *It's not really me,* he thought, *to be dressed up like this and in with a crowd like this. One day I'll be going to see the King of kings, and I won't need to hire a suit then, and when I do see him my beloved partner Norma will be beside me. Only we'll no longer be man and wife but brother and sister in Christ.* He sat down and let his eyes scan the beautiful room. The pictures and furniture were glorious and he was proud to be there and to accept the MBE, not only for himself, but also on behalf of all those at Manchester Prison. There had been many heroes during the riot, and many were unsung. The staff and chaplaincy team had been marvellous—and a lot of the inmates had also shown tremendous courage in helping the prison staff. Yes, he was accepting this Honour on behalf of all those who had shown such courage.

As he looked round quietly he could not help thinking back to all the experiences that had brought him to Buckingham Palace. He could see now in his mind's eye the smoke and flames billowing out of the old Strangeways roof and through the tiny cell windows. He could remember the taunts, cat calls and slates hurled down from the roof as staff and prisoners ran the gauntlet to escape. He could remember the total devastation in the chapel, everything smashed, his Bible soaked and ruined. He remembered that first Tuesday where he was hurting so bitterly inside that he couldn't even talk to Norma about it. He had driven home for lunch and found Norma and Sister Dominic in the lounge; Sister Dominic, the little Roman Catholic nun who came in to take classes in the prison. She had brought some flowers for Norma and as soon as he arrived her first words were, 'Noel, you have experienced your crucifixion. You have seen your flock scattered all over the place, to all the prisons throughout the country. Your work seems to have fallen in around you. You have had your tears, and your heartache, and your anguish, and you are suffering. But Noel, God has got a glorious resurrection for you—a resurrection that is greater than you can ever imagine.' And with that he had burst into tears. Perhaps it was then that he had begun to experience something of the healing power of tears. When he had taken her back down to the convent in the car, he came out of the convent, sat in the car and just sobbed. Perhaps that was when God really began to deal with him. Her words had comforted him and stayed with him in the years since the riot.

He remembered the months after the riot, when he had first realised how ill Norma was and how he had guessed and understood why she did not tell him. He had been so angry with God, not for taking Norma so much sooner than he had expected, because he knew everyone had to die and they had been given the wonderful eighteen bonus years to see their daughters grow up; but because of her suffering and the indignities of her illness when he had known how much it meant to her to keep her dignity. How he had shouted at God as he drove to Christie Hospital and how Norma had known and loved him and teased him ever so gently. 'God has a new ministry for you. Why don't you let him give it to you?'

Noel sat very quietly in the ante-room at Buckingham Palace. All around him was subdued laughter and well-bred voices and best suits. He only thought of Norma; she would have loved being with him today. He realised now that in her death God had been bringing him through the valley, through the darkness, through the experience where everything was falling in around him. He knew now what grief was about, and why people can be angry when they lose a loved one. Now he could understand about prisons within the personality and within people's own characters. He knew because he had been in a prison like that. And slowly, slowly God had let him realise that the prison door was unlocked and he had stepped out into a new freedom, a new discovery of faith.

Soon it was time for him to be led forward to take his place in the sedate queue of people who waited with suppressed excitement for their turn to be presented to

Her Majesty. When Noel caught a glimpse of her and then went forward, he saw that she was a little woman and that she had a flowery dress on. He found himself thinking that she was somehow not quite what he had expected her to be. He had imagined her in the grandeur and glitter of a state occasion, but now he realised that she was a human being, just the same as he was, as everybody was; that human nature is the same the world over.

He stepped forward and bowed. The Queen shook his hand and said, 'Chaplain of Strangeways, that must be a difficult job.'

Noel looked at her and said, 'We have our moments, Ma'am.'

Then she pinned his decoration to his lapel and shook his hand again. And that was the end of the interview. Noel backed away from her and heard the orchestra on the balcony playing 'Moon River'. That was one of the songs Norma had enjoyed listening to; she had always associated its romance with their relationship.

As he went to his plush gilt chair to watch the others, Noel could not help remembering the officer, James, whom he had visited in hospital. How he had sat on by the man's bedside and found himself wondering if there was life after death at all.

As he had listened in silence to that life-after-death story, somehow his own faith had been rekindled. James had done something for him that day in hospital that the Queen, in all the pomp and ceremony of royalty, could never do for him. He would have to think about these things again. It was almost too much to take in at the present. He turned round, caught Helen's eye and smiled.

On the way back in the train that day Noel was thinking how Her Majesty the Queen in her generosity had welcomed him to Buckingham Palace and given him a memento that was very precious to him. He was a Canon of Manchester Cathedral, now an MBE and had also received a commendation for bravery from the Home Secretary. He was proud, pleased and humbled to have received these Honours from his country and to have met the Queen. But he had to admit that none of these things meant as much to him as Jesus Christ did. They meant nothing in comparison to the preciousness of being able to lead one person to the Lord and see their life transformed.

None of it meant anything in comparison to his rediscovery of the Lord Jesus Christ in a way that he had never known him before. Jesus had taught him how to weep, how to smile and laugh again; he had taught him how to be lonely, and how to adjust to loneliness; he had taught him how to return to him and cry out to him.

God was teaching him in his mercy and by the ruthlessness of his love, that all things did indeed work together for good to those who were called according to his purpose, and that the reason for God's sometimes inexplicable way was that Noel was being conformed into the image of God's Son, Jesus Christ. He leaned back in his seat as the train travelled on towards Manchester and closed his eyes for a moment. 'Thank you, Lord,' he said. And he knew himself to be a man at peace.

Noel retires as a prison chaplain at Strangeways on 31st December 1995. However, he is not anticipating a quieter life. He has been granted by the Bishop a licence within the diocese of Manchester, and will be working with the Director of Evangelism, Canon Wilfred Gash. As a Canon of Manchester Cathedral he will also be working with the Cathedral in a pastoral role. His services have been accepted as a weekly voluntary chaplain at the North Manchester Hospital. And of course he will continue to be a member of his local church, St Paul's, Kersal Moor.

Sources

1. Noel's typed evidence as submitted and presented to the Woolf Enquiry (14th May 1990).
2. *The Observer* (8th April 1990).
3. *Church Times* (11th May 1990).
4. Many local papers from April–July 1990—useful mainly for pictures.
5. Noel's own recollections.
6. Video *Out of Darkness into Light*—John Whatmore/Media Services.
7. *Gatelodge*, Prison Officers' Magazine (June 1990).
8. Prison Service News (May 1990).
9. Norma's private journal.

Prison Pentecost

by Michael Apichella

When Michael Apichella began to hear that prisoners were being converted to Christianity at an unprecedented rate, he decided to visit as many prisons as would welcome him, to find out what was going on.

What he discovered is recorded in this book, and the facts speak for themselves.

Let this compelling account inspire you to pray and work for refreshing and revival for all those who are 'in prison' – whether locked in a physical cell or simply bound by the mistakes of the past.

'I think that God would like to see empty prisons.'
– Graham Dodds,
Channings Wood Chaplaincy Team

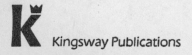

Kingsway Publications